HUNGRY HAPPENS: MEDITERRANEAN

100 Healthy, Simple Recipes

HUNGRY HAPPENS:
MEDITERRANEAN

Stella Drivas
with Lukas Volger

Photographs by Antonis Achilleos

Clarkson Potter/Publishers
New York

CLARKSON POTTER/PUBLISHERS
An imprint of the Crown Publishing Group
A division of Penguin Random House LLC
clarksonpotter.com
penguinrandomhouse.com

Copyright © 2025 by Stella Drivas
Photographs copyright © 2025 by Antonis Achilleos

Penguin Random House values and supports copyright. Copyright fuels creativity, encourages diverse voices, promotes free speech, and creates a vibrant culture. Thank you for buying an authorized edition of this book and for complying with copyright laws by not reproducing, scanning, or distributing any part of it in any form without permission. You are supporting writers and allowing Penguin Random House to continue to publish books for every reader. Please note that no part of this book may be used or reproduced in any manner for the purpose of training artificial intelligence technologies or systems.

CLARKSON POTTER is a trademark and **POTTER** with colophon is a registered trademark of Penguin Random House LLC.

Library of Congress Cataloging-in-Publication Data
Names: Drivas, Stella, author. | Volger, Lukas, author. | Achilleos, Antonis, photographer.
Title: Hungry happens, Mediterranean / by Stella Drivas with Lukas Volger ; photographs by Antonis Achilleos. Description: New York : Clarkson Potter/Publishers, [2025] | Includes index. | Identifiers: LCCN 2024052603 (print) | LCCN 2024052604 (ebook) | ISBN 9780593800416 (hardcover) | ISBN 9780593800423 (ebook) Subjects: LCSH: Cooking, Mediterranean. | LCGFT: Cookbooks.
Classification: LCC TX725.M35 D75 2025 (print) | LCC TX725.M35 (ebook) | DDC 641.59/1822—dc23/eng/20241205
LC record available at https://lccn.loc.gov/2024052603
LC ebook record available at https://lccn.loc.gov/2024052604

ISBN 978-0-593-80041-6
Ebook ISBN 978-0-593-80042-3

Editor: Susan Roxborough
Editorial assistant: Elaine Hennig
Art director: Ian Dingman
Production editor: Ashley Pierce
Production: Kelli Tokos
Production designer: Christina Self
Food stylist: Monica Pierini
Food stylist assistant: Alyssa Kondrack
Prop stylist: Paige Hicks
Recipe developers: Stella Drivas and Lukas Volger
Recipe tester: Julie Bishop
Copyeditor: Dolores York
Proofreaders: Robin Slutzky, Miriam Garron, and Surina Jain
Compositors: Merri Ann Morrell and Hannah Hunt
Indexer: Barbara Mortenson
Publicist: Kristin Casemore
Marketer: Chloe Aryeh

Manufactured in China

10 9 8 7 6 5 4 3 2 1

First Edition

The authorized representative in the EU for product safety and compliance is Penguin Random House Ireland, Morrison Chambers, 32 Nassau Street, Dublin D02 YH68, Ireland, https://eu-contact.penguin.ie.

FOR ELINA AND YIANNIS, WHOSE LOVE AND SUPPORT LIFT ME UP EVERY DAY

CONTENTS

- **9** Introduction: Love Your Life
- **15** Season with Your Soul

MORNINGS

- **29** Homemade Yogurt Flatbreads with Smoked Salmon, Avocado & Tzatziki
- **30** Veggie Egg Bites with Feta & Olives
- **33** Chocolate Chip & Banana Breakfast Cookies
- **34** Baba's Grain-Free Pancakes with Easy Fruit Compote
- **37** Cocoa Dutch Baby with Fresh Strawberries
- **38** Baked Egg Tortilla with Ham & Beans
- **41** Banana-Oat Bread with Blueberries
- **42** Veggie Quiche in a Smashed Potato Crust
- **45** Elina's Pumpkin–Chocolate Chip Muffins
- **46** Breakfast Biscuit Loaf

SUNSET MEZZE

- **51** Garidopetoules (Shrimp Fritters)
- **52** Sesame-Crusted Baked Feta with Hot Honey
- **55** Balsamic Roasted Strawberries with Whipped Honey-Ricotta
- **56** Melitzanosalata Garlic Bread (Cheesy Garlic Bread Topped with Greek Eggplant Dip)
- **59** Diner Cheeseburger Bites with Special Sauce
- **60** Air-Fryer Artichoke Bites with Aioli
- **63** Smashed Broccoli Chips with Spicy Ranch Dip
- **64** Baked Halloumi & Gouda in Puff Pastry
- **67** Crispy Feta-Stuffed Olives
- **68** Tahini-Crusted Chickpeas
- **71** Spinach & Feta Cookies
- **72** Spicy Salmon-Rice Muffins

HUNGRY IN A HURRY

- **77** Chicken Saganaki
- **78** Easy Lemon-Garlic-Parmesan Chicken
- **81** Creamy Lemon Shrimp & Zucchini
- **82** Boyfriend Steak Skillet with Peppers & Feta
- **85** Zucchini & Prosciutto "Lasagna" Loaf
- **86** Honey-Roasted Salmon-Farro Bowls with Radishes & Broccolini
- **89** Crunchy Baked Beef Souvlaki Tacos
- **90** Coastal Baked Cod
- **93** Seared Scallops over Creamy Zucchini Couscous
- **94** Mediterranean Meatloaf
- **97** Warm Winter Vegetable Salad with Quinoa
- **98** Broccoli-Feta Soup

GO GREEK

- **103** Loaf Pan Chicken Gyros
- **104** Chicken Fasolakia (Green Bean Stew)
- **107** Easier Skillet Moussaka
- **108** Yiannis's Favorite Pork Souvlaki Wraps
- **111** Soutzoukakia (Baked Meatballs & Potatoes)
- **112** Greek Lamb Fricassee
- **115** Deconstructed Gemista (Deconstructed Rice & Vegetable Stuffed Peppers)
- **116** Halibut Kleftiko (Pesto Halibut Baked in Parchment)
- **119** Fáva (Greek Split Pea Soup)
- **120** Arakas (Braised Sweet Peas with Artichokes & Chickpeas)
- **123** Avgolemono (Lemony Chicken Soup)
- **124** Lazy Spanakopita
- **127** Broccoli Kaltsounia (Broccoli Hand Pies)
- **129** Lahanopita Strifti (Spiral Pie with Cabbage & Feta)
- **133** Ladenia (Greek Village Pizza)

MEDITERRANEAN MEALS

- **137** Sheet Pan Chicken Caponata
- **138** Honey-Butter Orange Roasted Chicken with Root Vegetables
- **141** Spicy Poached Salmon
- **142** One-Pan Chicken Orzo with Sun-Dried Tomatoes & Mozzarella
- **145** Creamy Sheet Pan Gnocchi
- **146** Lemony Orzotto with Spinach & Peas
- **149** Epic Meat Lasagna
- **150** Broccoli-Feta Pasta Bake
- **153** Smoky Spanish Lentil Soup with Chorizo
- **154** Crunchy Potato Schiacciata
- **157** Leek & Zucchini Scarpaccia
- **158** Herby Ricotta Dumplings in Vegetable Soup
- **161** Euro Tortellini Salad

CARB LIGHT

- **165** Low-Carb Chicken Nuggets with Crispy Baked French Fries
- **166** Vegetable-Stuffed Chicken Breasts
- **169** Mediterranean Turkey-Crust Pizza
- **170** Spinach & Feta Stuffed Salmon
- **173** Seaside Tuna Tostadas
- **174** Chili-Lime Shrimp "Tacos" with Pineapple Salsa
- **177** Roasted Veggie "Pizza"
- **178** Vegetable-Stuffed Portobellos
- **181** Creamy Zucchini & White Bean Soup
- **182** Roasted Garlic Girl Soup
- **185** Micro Chop Salad with Goddess Dressing
- **186** The Ultimate Cobb Salad

ON THE SIDE

- **191** Fresh Zucchini Noodle Salad
- **192** Spiced Tahini Squash with Lime & Feta
- **195** Greek Layered Potato Bake
- **196** Cauliflower Steaks Parmesan
- **199** Roasted Pesto Cabbage Wedges
- **200** Crispy Parmesan Carrot Sticks with Lazy Tzatziki
- **203** Mediterranean Veggie Stir-Fry
- **204** Spiced Roasted Asparagus over Burrata
- **207** Honey-Balsamic Roasted Beets
- **208** Horiatiki (Classic Greek Salad over White Bean–Feta Whip)
- **211** Summery Pita Salad with Figs, Peaches, Tomatoes & Corn
- **212** Fall Brussels Sprouts Salad with Halloumi, Dates & Crispy Shallots
- **215** Cauliflower Wedge Salad with Bacon & Blue Cheese Dressing
- **216** Yiayia's Maroulosalata (Romaine Salad with Scallions & Dill)

SWEET SPOT

- **221** No-Bake Strawberry Tiramisu
- **222** Mama's Juicy Fruit Salad
- **225** Lighter Baklava Cheesecake Bars
- **226** Vegan Tahini–Chocolate Chunk Cookies
- **229** Bougatsa Cups (Custard Pie Bites)
- **230** Mom's Vasilopita (New Year's Day Yogurt Cake)
- **233** Portokalopita (Orange Phyllo Cake)
- **234** Flexible Peanut Butter–Banana Chocolate Chip Bars
- **237** Invisible Apple Loaf Cake
- **238** No-Bake Brownie Cups
- **241** Easy Coconut Cake
- **242** Five-Minute Sangria Slushie

- **244** Nutritional Information
- **249** Acknowledgments
- **250** Index

INTRODUCTION: LOVE YOUR LIFE

Every day in the kitchen, I'm guided by two convictions. The first is that *cooking is one of life's greatest pleasures*. This was true for my parents, my grandparents, and likely all of my Greek ancestors, because for us food and cooking have been practically everything: nourishment, connection, work, heritage—and pleasure, of course.

I enjoy the process in its entirety. I love grocery shopping, surveying all the ingredients to find what speaks to me, and even unloading my purchases at home, because I'm comforted by the knowledge of delicious meals to come. Then there's the full sensory experience in the kitchen—washing, slicing, chopping, cooking, baking, seasoning—I'm engaged by it all. But the best part comes at the end, because I take great satisfaction in sharing a home-cooked meal with my family and loved ones.

The second conviction is that *homemade food is always better*. This is something I learned firsthand, growing up in a house where we ate only from-scratch meals, made with fresh, healthy ingredients and lots of love.

My parents arrived in the United States as immigrants with practically nothing, and there were many years when our family didn't have many material possessions. But we were always well fed at home. This experience gave me a deep and profound appreciation for the power of a healthful, home-cooked meal and how it is one of the deepest expressions of love one person can show for another.

Every day I marvel at my luck that I grew up this way, and for the opportunity I've had to continue my family's legacy of food through Hungry Happens, the website and content platform I created. I consider it such a privilege to cook in my kitchen, to enjoy these meals with my family and community—and now, to share with you this book that's full of so many treasured recipes.

MY GREEK ROOTS

My parents and grandparents all came from Sparta, in the Peloponnesus region of Greece, where a very different pace of life prevailed over what most of us know now. There weren't supermarkets to shop at, cars to drive, or many of the distractions that dominate so much of our lives today. Their days revolved around their community, with food as the anchor.

Of course, things weren't perfect. There was a lot of instability in Greece at the time, following a military coup that began in 1967. Between the political situation and the promise of the American dream, my parents separately immigrated to the United States, each with the equivalent of a sixth-grade education, determined to create better, more prosperous lives for themselves and their future children.

My parents met in the United States, and within two months of knowing each other, they married and got started building a family among a small community of other Greek immigrants on Long Island, New York. My dad found work as a baker at a restaurant, making cookies, pies, tarts, and cakes. He may not have realized it at the time, but this job was the beginning of my family's long-lasting profession in food.

My parents felt a lot of pressure during that period as they worked so hard to create a stable, secure home. As anyone who starts from scratch must do, they made endless sacrifices, taking risks they weren't sure would pay off, and worked nonstop to save for a better future for us. We lived very modestly, at first because we had so little, and over time, because my parents saved almost every penny they earned. Having grown up poor, they knew how to stretch a dollar as much as possible, and they were experts at finding the best prices. My father always used to say, "It's not how much you make, but how much you save that counts the most." Slowly they established financial stability, realizing their American dream by ultimately becoming owners of Greek diners in New York that they operated for thirty-five years. To say that my dad was dedicated to his businesses is a gross understatement.

My maternal grandparents lived with us while I was growing up, and if you've ever seen *My Big Fat Greek Wedding*, it was kind of like that. Everything was a family affair, and my family was a huge presence in my life, in particular my yiayia (what we call our grandmothers in Greek), Dimitra. While my parents were working around the clock, she made it her responsibility to create a warm, safe home that was overflowing with love and kindness. Yiayia always made sure that I felt an abundance of care and attention.

And food was absolutely Yiayia's love language. She was an incredible cook, who made everything from scratch. Neither she nor my parents conformed to the American style of eating, with a new diet in vogue every other week and a prevalence of processed foods. She cooked with fresh ingredients, never using canned foods or frozen vegetables. (Not that there's anything wrong with these things—she just never touched them. We never even had canned soup at home!) Yiayia brought the Greek food traditions she'd learned from her mother and grandmother, passing our family's recipes down to me so that future generations wouldn't forget.

There were always abundant fresh fruits and vegetables. Bread was always homemade, not store-bought. Every meal was balanced. She was intent on keeping us connected to our heritage. While I may not have appreciated every one of those classic Greek dishes as a kid, as an adult, I now recognize that time as a stroke of unbelievable luck. With a role model like Yiayia, who wouldn't ultimately fall in love with healthy Greek food?

MY HEALTHY EATING JOURNEY

Because we were in the restaurant business, my family rarely went out to eat. Instead, my parents insisted we eat home-cooked meals at every opportunity, and my dad always stressed the importance of staying away from prepared and highly processed foods. When I wanted a snack or dessert after dinner, fresh fruit was the sole option, never chips or candy or anything actually dessert-ish. Combined with Yiayia's classic Greek cooking, this was the foundation of my culinary education.

In the ensuing years as an adult, my relationship with food went through many changes. I gained and lost weight with both my pregnancies, experimenting with every method of exerting control that I could think of: from starving myself (which I absolutely do not recommend) and very strict dieting, to intense exercise regimens and various elimination programs centered on "clean" eating.

Everyone has their own health journey, and for those seeking to hit specific goals, I know what it's like. I'm not here to judge or shame. Goals require discipline, both in food and in life (in my kitchen/office you'll find the saying "Discipline is freedom" tacked up on the wall!).

But for everyone simply aiming to maintain their health and have a low-stress relationship with what they eat, what I've ultimately come to realize is that moderation is the golden ticket. And in this way, Hungry Happens represents a relationship with food that's quite different from what I've known through the peaks and valleys of my adult life. I've learned how to fine-tune my cooking with healthy ingredients and balanced meals, while also satisfying my cravings and enjoying all the recipes I now want to share.

So when people ask me about my tricks for staying healthy when I spend all day in the kitchen making such delicious food, I tell them that it pretty much comes down to this: Stop eating when you're 80 percent full. I've been the happiest and most satisfied during the periods of my life when I've been able to abide by this rule.

Of course, *what* I eat factors in here in a big way, too, and that's what makes Hungry Happens something of a full-circle moment. Like my yiayia and my parents, I'm an advocate for homemade meals—a hundred times out of ten, they're going to be healthier than any of the more convenient options that might seem so enticing in the heat of the moment. And like them, fresh fruits and vegetables are central to my diet. I always try to balance out my plate with protein, fiber, and healthy fats, using recognizable, nonprocessed foods.

In general, you can't beat Mediterranean cuisine when it comes to healthy eating. It delivers delicious, full-flavored meals that prioritize fresh ingredients that are beneficial for all-around good health. Study after study supplies more evidence that if you want to live longer and feel good, eat a diet rich in olive oil, lean proteins and healthy fats, and plenty of fruits and vegetables. It isn't very complicated.

And a final, foundational element of healthy eating that I learned directly from my grandparents and parents: Nobody is perfect! You must also make sure to enjoy the things you love. One of my papou's (my grandfather's) favorite meals was a McDonald's cheeseburger—he treated himself to it once a week. My dad, on the other hand, would never eat McDonald's, but he sure had a sweet tooth and had to indulge it every now and then with a cookie or bite of cake. Like my dad, I have a sweet tooth, too, and I honor it occasionally with ice cream, homemade chocolate chip cookies, or a cup of hot cocoa. While making healthy choices is important, you've got to enjoy your life, too.

THE STORY OF HUNGRY HAPPENS

I've dreamed of writing a cookbook for many years, but it's been a roundabout path to get here. Around 2013, I was seeing a lot of people sharing recipes online, and I thought, "I can do that!" For a little while, I considered what to call a food venture of my own, mulling over numerous possibilities until the phrase hungry . . . happens! came to me out of the blue one night while I was watching TV. It was simple and succinct, and I haven't looked back since.

At that time, I was focused on "clean" eating, and many of the recipes I shared were somewhat different from what I'm known for now. I built a following and connected with so many amazing people, but after a few years, I decided to reexamine my purpose and figure out what I really wanted to share when it comes to food. I put a pause on Hungry Happens and went back to my day job working out of an office.

When I returned to Hungry Happens, I was ready to fine-tune its focus. I wanted to share my journey of learning how to cook easy, healthy meals at home for me and my kids, using real, fresh, good-for-you ingredients that aren't difficult to find, and to draw from many of the Greek and Mediterranean influences that have shaped my life. It was important to me that everything be both simple *and* delicious—because that's how I like to cook! One recipe at a time, my vision started to come to life, and a food-loving, international community of people who are just as excited as I am by doable, healthy recipes with some Greek and Mediterranean flair found its way to my work.

In order to fully realize my vision, I needed to create a proper website so that all my recipes would have a home. At the time, I wasn't earning a lot of money, so I asked my dad if he'd help me with a loan to cover the cost of building it. He obliged, and I promised to pay him back as soon as I could. I'll never forget how he replied: "You only have to pay me back if it *isn't* successful."

It makes me very emotional to share this. Only a few years later, in 2022, he passed away. But he was there to watch Hungry Happens catch on and become my career, and he gave his stamp of approval to so many of my most beloved recipes. He was so proud of me.

It strikes me now as so *him* to have created that condition on his loan, expressing his belief in me and my capabilities, but also motivating me to put the work in. There's not a day that I don't think of him, especially as I continue to grow Hungry Happens and through the process of writing this cookbook. Starting from nothing, he made so many sacrifices to create this opportunity for me, making my dream a reality.

WHAT TO EXPECT FROM THIS BOOK

My goal with this cookbook is to share with you my conviction that homemade is always better!—and through my recipes, to show you how truly attainable it is to make healthy, delicious meals at home.

The recipe chapters span the day—from breakfast through dessert—but the focus is strongly on what to make for dinner. There are plenty of quick one-pan chicken dishes, low-carb spins on pizza (see pages 133 and 169) and tacos (see page 174), meal-worthy soups and salads—not to mention many of the classic Greek dishes I've been eating my whole life. I guarantee that these are recipes the entire family will indulge in.

You'll also find a whole chapter of some of the unique side dishes I'm known for, like Crispy Parmesan Carrot Sticks (page 200) and Roasted Pesto Cabbage Wedges (page 199). And there are the baked treats, both savory and sweet, that I know you will love, many of them created with health in mind: lower in carbs, and featuring good, whole, healthy fats and other nutrient-rich ingredients.

For a recipe to earn its place in my cookbook, it had to pass the "wow" test. It had to have something special that makes it so delicious that you'll never forget it. And of course, it also had to be straightforward and easy. If you'd like nutritional info for each of these recipes, you'll find it collected in the appendix on page 244.

My aim is to help you find the entire process of cooking and sharing meals with your family and friends as fulfilling as I do. So thank you for coming with me on what I hope will also be an incredibly rewarding journey for you—that these family-favorite recipes of mine will become favorites of yours, too, and that they will find a place in your busy but delicious lives.

Now it's time to start cooking. So put on your apron, grab a cutting board, and get ready to *love your life*.

Stella

SEASON
WITH
YOUR
SOUL

Cooking healthy, homemade meals on a regular basis is not hard. For me, the most important part is approaching it as a daily practice and as an activity to bring intention and all my awareness to. When I first started making cooking videos, I often used the phrase "season with your soul." The idea still guides me because I most enjoy being in the kitchen when I'm fully in the moment, guided by my instincts, appetite, and all the wonderful sensory details.

That said, there is always a clear set of parameters in mind. The first is that I make sure my recipes are straightforward and easy, with no unnecessary steps or extra dishes that can turn the pleasure into a chore. The second is that I rely on keeping my pantry well stocked with an assortment of healthy, go-to ingredients that can be the basis for any number of meals.

MY GREEK PANTRY

It's so easy to cook like a Greek, because the cuisine has few, though specific, staple ingredients. Here are the essentials that are worth keeping on hand for my recipes.

Greek olive oil. The healthiest, most delicious fat around. Use the best quality you can afford and use it liberally—both for cooking and for drizzling, and even as medicine! I'm very partial to olive oil from the Peloponnesus region of Greece, which is where I'm from, and I always buy it in big 3-liter cans that I decant into an oil cruet for day-to-day use.

Greek feta and other cheeses. No Greek meal—breakfast, lunch, dinner, or even dessert—is complete without a big hunk of feta at the table. Buy brine-packed feta from Greece, avoiding anything that's in shrink-wrapped plastic or, even worse, precrumbled. When feta is in one of my recipes, I always list the measurement in ounces rather than cups or tablespoons, and I do this because I think it's easier to use the package weight as a guide when trimming off a piece to crumble into what you're cooking. Other cheeses that are mainstays in Greece but can be trickier to find in the United States include kefalotiri, graviera, kasseri, kefalograviera, and anthotyro.

Lemons. Every Greek kitchen has a big bowl of lemons on display, because freshly squeezed lemon juice goes in just about everything: fish and meat marinades, salad dressings, vegetables, rice, and, of course, to flavor desserts. I always look for organic lemons and give them a squeeze to make sure they're heavy and full of juice.

Garlic. In Greece, garlic is dosed out like medicine as a cure-all for whatever ails you, from a sore throat to an immunity booster. How lucky that it's also so delicious.

Whole milk Greek yogurt. Yogurt is a staple of breakfasts and baking and is used in marinades to tenderize meat. I always buy full-fat whole milk yogurt, and if I'm unfamiliar with a brand, the first thing I do is check the ingredients to make sure there's nothing more than milk and live cultures in there, steering clear of added sugar, stabilizers, and other additives.

Fresh herbs. Our mainstay herbs are mint, parsley, oregano, dill, and basil, and we use much more than just a little sprinkle here and there. We add handfuls of sharp, fragrant flavor to salads, bakes, and savory pies. I always wash extra for garnishing, too.

Fresh vegetables and fruits. The cornerstone of any healthy diet, especially Greek and Mediterranean ones, is fresh fruits and vegetables, and my kitchen is always overflowing with them. I buy locally grown organic produce whenever possible.

Good olives. You'll find a medley of olives—including my favorite Kalamata olives, Castelvetranos, and Frescatranos—eaten throughout Greece, either alongside fresh bread and cheese, served in salads, or used as accents to fillings and main entrées. Generally, it's better to buy olives with the pits still in them, and if where you live, there's an olive bar that has plenty of turnover, that's where you'll find olives with optimal freshness. Otherwise, brine-packed olives will keep for a long time.

Nuts and seeds. Greek and Mediterranean cuisine is full of various nuts and seeds, including almonds, walnuts, and sesame seeds that show up often in these recipes in the form of crunchy toppings, fillings, and garnishes, and ground into flour for baking as well.

Honey. Greek cooks are masters of combining sweet and savory (see my Sesame-Crusted Baked Feta with Hot Honey on page 52). Honey comes into play as a sweetener but also as a drizzle for cheese and yogurt, in dressings and marinades, and to add a little complexity of flavor and contrast to meat dishes as well. I prefer locally sourced, raw, and runny honey for most of my cooking.

MY HEALTH-FORWARD PANTRY

My day-to-day diet is a blend of the Greek foods I grew up with, as well as this more explicitly health-oriented roster of ingredients that keeps me feeling my best.

Eggs. A mainstay of my diet, eggs are very important to me. They provide a complete protein, healthy fat, vital nutrients and minerals, and a yummy richness you can't get anywhere else. They're prominent in my baking, and I only buy organic, pasture-raised eggs. And as a quick meal, I typically cook them with any veggies that are on hand and half an avocado on the side, sprinkled with either salt or everything bagel seasoning.

Animal proteins. While I love my vegetables, I greatly depend on animal proteins, including chicken, beef, lamb, and pork, and fish and shellfish to keep me feeling satiated and healthy. When shopping for meat, I look for indicators of care regarding animal welfare and nutrition, opting for free-range, grass-fed, wild-caught, and pastured meats and seafood whenever possible.

Plant proteins. I often reach for beans as far as plant proteins go, with my favorites being lentils, chickpeas, and black beans. These are easy to add to salads, soups, and even to use as creative garnishes (see my Tahini-Crusted Chickpeas on page 68).

Whole milk dairy. I grew up drinking a glass of milk every day (to which my mother attributes my tall height), and I only do full-fat dairy, never choosing low-fat or fat-free versions of things like milk, sour cream, yogurt, or cottage cheese. I believe dairy to be an extremely healthful, wholesome ingredient, and I often use unsalted butter, whole milk, and heavy cream in my cooking and baking.

My holy quartet of dried herbs. Onion powder, garlic powder, Italian herb blend, and paprika appear frequently in these recipes!

Celtic sea salt. I am a huge fan of fine-grain Celtic sea salt for its fuller flavor and the trace minerals it contains. I even travel with it. If you cook with coarse salt, such as kosher salt, taste as you go. Generally, coarse salt should be doubled if substituting it for fine salt.

Tahini. I love the rich, unique flavor of tahini and am always coming up with excuses to incorporate it into my baking and cooking, adding it to sauces, dressings, and baked goods, and smearing it over toast as a snack or quick breakfast. Always check the expiration date to find the freshest possible tahini when shopping for it.

Almond flour and oat flour. In gluten-free baking, I often use superfine almond flour and oat flour in place of all-purpose wheat flour, preferring them over a gluten-free flour blend. If you are following a strict gluten-free diet, be sure to buy oats and oat flour labeled "certified gluten-free." And if you don't have oat flour, you can always just process rolled oats in a blender until they're finely ground. And I highly recommend using almond flour in place of bread crumbs if you need a gluten-free, low-carb crumb coating.

Natural sweeteners. Honey and maple syrup appear more often in my baking than granulated white sugar.

Cheese. I am a cheese girl! In addition to the Greek cheeses listed above, I cook with Parmesan cheese, as well as mozzarella, sharp Cheddar, and Mexican blend in all kinds of savory recipes. For many of these cheeses, I opt for blocks that I grate myself to avoid the caking agents used in preshredded cheese. I also love more specialty cheeses like blue cheese, goat cheese, Gruyère, and fontina, and I often incorporate cottage cheese into various recipes for an added protein boost.

Medjool dates. Dates are nature's candy. They're not only delicious as a sweet caramel-flavored treat but are also full of fiber, iron, and antioxidants. A perfect snack if you've got a sweet tooth, I also love adding them to salads, desserts, and fruit plates.

THE VALUE OF COMMUNITY

In Greek culture, community is everything. Shared meals and tables are the cornerstones of the day, and cooking is just as valued, too, as time spent with family, neighbors, and loved ones. Even though so much of modern life wants us to be in solitude, I always make sure to treat food as togetherness. Similarly, in my work with Hungry Happens, it is the community that's found my recipes—of other home cooks and lovers of Greek and Mediterranean cuisine—that keep me excited to show up every single day!

WHAT I EAT IN A DAY

While every meal is important in Greek culture, dinner was typically the main event in my family, and it was always composed of a main and several side dishes. Dinner still tends to be the more involved meal of the day for me and my kids, but unlike Yiayia and my mom, my style is to keep things easy. And breakfasts and lunches are always quick and easy, too. Here's how an average day of eating looks for me.

Breakfast is simple. Most days I start with a cup of bone broth or, occasionally, a cup of Greek coffee. My kids and I will eat a quick, savory baked dish like the Baked Egg Tortilla (page 38), or if my daughter, Elina, has made her Pumpkin–Chocolate Chip Muffins (page 45), we will toast and drizzle them with tahini. In the summer, I love a classic Greek breakfast of good Greek yogurt, topped with fresh fruit, tahini, and a light drizzle of honey.

Quick and light lunch. Lunch is often a quickly assembled meal for me, consisting of a few soft-boiled or poached eggs with fresh vegetables and avocado. Or it might be a scoop of tuna fish salad or cottage cheese, served on lettuce leaves, with vegetables alongside.

"All-inclusive" main for dinner. Recipes like my Vegetable-Stuffed Chicken Breasts (page 166) and Coastal Baked Cod (page 90) combine protein and vegetables, making them a one-stop shop, needing only a simple side such as Yiayia's Maroulosalata (page 216), freshly cooked rice or cauliflower rice, or some crusty bread to mop up juices. Other meals, like Loaf Pan Chicken Gyros (page 103), served with warm pitas and various toppings, or Crunchy Baked Beef Souvlaki Tacos (page 89), are interactive mains, involving toppings and condiments that allow everyone to customize their own plates at the table.

Occasional dessert. Everyone in my family has a sweet tooth, including me, and sometimes after dinner, we'll have a dessert that's lower in sugar and carbs than the traditional version, such as Vegan Tahini–Chocolate Chunk Cookies (page 226) or my Lighter Baklava Cheesecake Bars (page 225) if they're on hand. But more often, we will do as I did while growing up, which is to cleanse our palates with fresh fruit, reserving more elaborate desserts for special occasions.

Meal prepping and leftovers. Growing up, the cooks in my family never meal-prepped (my yiayia was essentially our short-order cook, making us whatever we wanted on request—not how I do it with my kids!). If I'm feeling organized, meal prepping is something that helps me a lot in my work on the Hungry Happens website. I'll get ahead of produce prep, map out a schedule for my cooking when I know I'll have more free time, and sometimes I'll make more involved dishes like my Epic Meat Lasagna (page 149) and stash them away in the freezer. Sometimes it works for me, sometimes it doesn't. But I always pack up my leftovers so that they don't go to waste. I get so happy when I open my fridge and find ready-to-go meals waiting. This gives me a much-needed night off.

EIGHT RULES FOR BETTER EVERYDAY COOKING

On a day-to-day basis, these rules always ensure that cooking is enjoyable and stress-free.

1 Read the recipe fully. Before you start cooking, read the recipe in its entirety—at least once, if not twice. In the end, this always saves me time, and it prevents unnecessary mistakes when I'm cooking.

2 Use quality ingredients. The sum of a cooked dish is only as great as its individual parts, and I believe that using the best ingredients you can get your hands on is super important for creating delicious meals. In everything from proteins, produce, and olive oil, all the way to my dried herbs, I always prioritize freshness and flavor. It makes a real difference.

3 Embrace mise en place. You probably know this is a French term that means "everything in its place." For me, it means taking a few minutes to clear away a workspace, gathering my ingredients and tools, and starting cooking from a mindset of feeling prepared. It makes cooking more controlled and therapeutic, setting me up for success. This is a good approach to all aspects of life, really.

4 Season properly. So often when something tastes a little lackluster, there just isn't enough salt. It's gotten a bad rap, but seasoning isn't so much about making things taste salty as it is about making all the other flavors pop. Taste often and season as you go, according to your own taste buds. And when it comes to meat, my general seasoning rule is: 1 teaspoon of fine sea salt per 1 pound of meat.

5 Be present and creative. In Greece, cooking was often the day's primary activity for my yiayia, involving numerous family members. It was as much an event as it was a functional task. For me, being present is key to ensuring that cooking is pleasurable and low stress. This involves tasting as I go to make sure flavors are balanced, including my kids in the process as much as possible, and overall, making sure to savor the whole experience.

6 Cook to temperature, not to time. I strongly recommend investing in a probe-style digital meat thermometer, which takes a lot of guesswork out of cooking meat. And in general, it's important to remember that there are a lot of variables when it comes to home cooking, so all cooks must learn to trust their instincts. "High heat" might be stronger on your stovetop compared to mine, for example. Use my suggested cooking times as guides but let your senses be the real authorities.

7 Don't skip the garnish! I love to add garnishes, and throughout these recipes, you'll see that almost every recipe includes a garnish of some sort. A pop of color or heat, a fresh and fragrant scattering of herbs, a drizzle of good Greek olive oil, or even a wedge of lemon to spritz at the table—these are things that help make a dish visually interesting and feel complete.

8 Cleanup is key. I love to do the dishes while things are baking or cooking—it's the perfect downtime to clean up; this lightens the load after eating. And it always takes less time than I expect it to. There's just no better feeling than waking up in the morning to a clean kitchen.

SEASON WITH YOUR SOUL

FIVE HEALTH RULES I LIVE BY

I've experimented with several different styles of healthy eating over the course of my adult life. But where I've ultimately landed with Hungry Happens is simple rather than strict and close in spirit to the way I ate growing up, too.

1 **Avoid processed foods.** This was one of my dad's cardinal rules, and I follow it just as strictly as he did. I operate by the axiom that if you don't recognize it or can't pronounce what you see on an ingredient list, then it's probably best to avoid it.

2 **Watch out for red flags.** I avoid any foods that have these types of claims plastered on their labels: *Low-Fat, Naturally Flavored, Lowers Cholesterol, Sugar-Free, All-Natural, Fat-Free,* and *Enriched*. And the reason for this is—see Rule Number 1. These words are signals to me that there are a lot of chemicals and other additives in there.

3 **Limit flour, sugar, and carbs.** I love bread, and it's a huge part of my Greek culture, but I tend to reserve it for the dishes that really need it—hearty soups like my Broccoli-Feta Soup (page 98) and saucy meals that need something for mopping up all that flavor, like my Greek Lamb Fricassee (page 112)—and for special occasions, rather than simply putting it on the table for every meal. This extends to all-purpose flour, simple carbs like rice and pasta, and sugar. The same goes for dessert. In my family and in Greek culture generally, cakes, cookies, and pies are reserved for special occasions rather than for an every-night kind of thing. My favorite carbohydrates are vegetables, and when I have a hankering for a sweet, I typically reach for fresh fruit.

4 **Prioritize fiber, protein, and healthy fats.** These are really the pillars of health and the basis for a balanced diet, as far as I'm concerned. When I sit down to eat, I first eat my high-fiber food, because it's satiating and prevents a glucose spike. Next is the protein, followed by the healthy fat. Starch is last, because by this point in the meal, I can rest easy knowing that I won't fill up on it. If I eat dessert, I always have it at the end of my meal, never as a snack or standalone thing, separate from the rest of my eating.

5 **And pile on the veggies!** You just can't go wrong if you've got an ample serving of vegetables at every meal, and in my recipes, I'm always trying to squeeze in more of them. For vitamins, minerals, fiber, and so many other nutrients, no picture of health is complete unless there is a bunch of fresh vegetables in there.

MY FIVE DAILY HEALTH TIPS

Here are a few health-related routines that my mother taught me and that I swear by.

1. **A small spoonful of mānuka honey.** Mānuka honey has many health benefits, including anti-inflammatory and antibacterial properties, so I have a small spoonful every day. I find that it can often help mitigate specific ailments in the moment, too, such as indigestion, nausea, or a headache.

2. **Lemon juice.** When I have a sore throat, I gargle with a bit of lemon juice. It always helps!

3. **A daily tablespoon of olive oil.** Like garlic, olive oil is as much a health remedy as it is a prominent ingredient throughout Greece. First thing in the morning and on an empty stomach, I always slurp a tablespoon of olive oil. It's rich in antioxidants, heart-healthy fats, and has many anti-inflammatory properties, so I do this for overall good health.

4. **Salt water oral rinse.** After brushing and flossing my teeth every night, I gargle with a bit of salt water. I find that it helps reduce plaque and inflammation in the mouth.

5. **Beef bone broth.** I love bone broth in the morning and drink it almost every day. It's an extra boost of protein, good for my gut health, my skin, and for keeping sickness at bay—and it's as satisfying, if not more, than a morning cup of coffee.

HOW TO USE THIS BOOK

Change It Up. Whether you're out of a certain ingredient or have a dietary restriction or preference, I know how important it is for recipes to be flexible. Throughout this book, I've added suggestions for changing up recipes with different types of vegetables, proteins, or flavor directions. Look for the heading Change It Up at the end of many of my recipes for easy customizations.

Gluten-free swaps. While I'm not gluten-free myself, I don't bake with all-purpose flour all that often, instead preferring more nutrient-dense almond or oat flours. In most instances, you can simply use one of these substitutes without worry or swap in your favorite one-to-one gluten-free flour blend. In place of conventional bread crumbs, use almond meal or store-bought gluten-free bread crumbs.

Dairy-free swaps. As I said, I love my cheese! It's one of my favorite ingredients, and it appears often in my recipes. If you don't eat dairy for some reason, you can sometimes simply leave the cheese out to make many of these either dairy-free or vegan. Nutritional yeast makes a great substitute for Parmesan cheese.

Sweeteners. Most of the time, I bake with honey or maple syrup rather than granulated sugar, but they may be used interchangeably.

Icons. Each recipe includes the following icons, indicating whether it is Vegetarian (VT), Vegan (VE), or Gluten-Free (GF). For recipes like desserts, where you can be safe to assume that they're vegetarian, I've left the Vegetarian icon out (though these will be called out if they're Gluten-Free or Vegan).

Nutrition information. For those who wish to find the nutritional information, you'll find it collected in an appendix at the back of the book on page 244, organized alphabetically by recipe name.

Cooking times. Approximate cooking times are included for each recipe, but they primarily encompass the active parts, such as prepping vegetables or cooking a dish in the oven. They do not factor in the time needed for marinating meats, for example, or the time it might take to make a separate recipe that's cross referenced and meant to be incorporated as a condiment, such as Lazy Tzatziki (page 200).

And with that, let's start cooking!

SEASON WITH YOUR SOUL

MORNINGS

More often than not, breakfast needs to come together pretty quickly at my house, because everyone is in a rush to get out the door. Things that can be prepped in advance like my Veggie Egg Bites (page 30) or Chocolate Chip & Banana Breakfast Cookies (page 33) are extra handy in these moments because they can be eaten on the go. But equally important, regardless of how much time we have, is that the first meal of the day be energizing and satiating! So, I make sure there's plenty of protein, that my morning baked goods are full of fiber and nutrient-rich grains, and loaded up with healthy fats and nut butters. The recipes in this chapter are the morning meals we keep on repeat, guaranteed to fuel the full day ahead.

HOMEMADE YOGURT FLATBREADS
with Smoked Salmon, Avocado & Tzatziki

You can easily make fresh, fluffy, homemade flatbreads from just a couple pantry ingredients and 30 minutes of your time, and in this recipe you'll make enough for a few meals. While they're perfect for wrapping around fillings and scooping up dips, they're a real treat at breakfast in this Mediterranean spin on my favorite bagel order. If you don't have time to make the flatbreads, store-bought pitas can easily be substituted.

Makes 4 breakfast toasts
Ready in 30 minutes

2 Yogurt Flatbreads (recipe follows) or store-bought pita breads
½ cup Lazy Tzatziki (page 200)
4 ounces lox (smoked salmon), sliced thinly
1 large avocado, sliced
¼ cup Favorite Pickled Red Onions (page 119)
Capers, for garnish
Chopped fresh dill, for garnish
Grated lemon zest, for garnish
Greek olive oil, for drizzling

Change It Up
Baked or Air-Fried Flatbreads: Cook the flatbreads in the oven or air fryer, arranging as many as will fit in an even layer, at 400°F for 12 to 14 minutes, flipping them halfway through.

Gluten-Free Flatbreads: Substitute almond flour or your favorite gluten-free flour blend for the all-purpose flour.

Note: I often roll out the dough portions and use a dinner plate as a guide and a pizza cutter to cut them into perfect rounds that fit my skillet (you can reroll the trimmings to make more flatbreads).

1. In a toaster or in a dry skillet on the stovetop, toast the flatbreads until they're just warmed through.

2. Cut each one in half through the diameter to create four half-moons. Spread each toasted flatbread with about 2 tablespoons tzatziki. Dividing evenly, top with the lox, avocado, and onions. Garnish with the capers, dill, and lemon zest, and drizzle the tops with the oil.

YOGURT FLATBREADS
Note that while I typically don't use fat-free or low-fat yogurt, it's necessary in this dough to achieve the right texture.
Makes 8 flatbreads

3 cups all-purpose flour, plus more for dusting
3¾ teaspoons baking powder
¾ teaspoon fine sea salt
1½ cups fat-free or 2% Greek yogurt
Greek olive oil, for frying

1. In a large bowl, whisk together the flour, baking powder, and salt. Stir in the yogurt, using a wooden spoon, then turn out the dough onto a clean work surface and knead the mixture into a smooth dough, about 5 minutes.

2. On a lightly floured work surface, divide the dough into eight equal portions, covering the rolled doughs with a clean kitchen towel to prevent them from drying out. Roll out each piece into a very thin round or oval (see Note). It's important that the dough portions be rolled thinly so they cook evenly.

3. Preheat a medium cast-iron skillet or other heavy medium skillet over medium-high heat. When hot, swirl in a splash of oil. Carefully lay one flatbread in the pan and cook until golden brown patches develop on the bottom, 2 to 3 minutes. Flip and repeat on the opposite side. Wrap the flatbread in a clean kitchen towel to keep it warm as you repeat this process for the remaining dough portions.

4. The flatbreads are best when they're freshly cooked, but when wrapped loosely at room temperature, they'll keep for about 2 days, or a month in the freezer, in an airtight bag or container.

VEGGIE EGG BITES
with Feta & Olives

The sous vide egg bites you can get at Starbucks are convenient, but they're also easy to make at home and are perfect for anyone aiming to prioritize protein in the morning. This recipe features some of my go-to vegetables, but it's easily customizable and a great recipe for meal-prepping breakfasts. Just be sure to bake them in a water bath, or bain-marie, because the gentler heat is critical to achieving a dense, creamy texture.

Makes 12 egg bites
Ready in 35 minutes

Butter or olive oil cooking spray, for greasing the muffin tin
2 teaspoons Greek olive oil
1 medium zucchini (6 to 8 ounces), finely diced
½ red bell pepper, diced small
2 scallions, green and white parts, thinly sliced
½ teaspoon red chile flakes
Fine sea salt and freshly ground black pepper
¼ cup chopped fresh dill or parsley
6 large eggs
1 cup whole milk cottage cheese
2 tablespoons potato starch or cornstarch
2 ounces Greek feta cheese, crumbled (about ½ cup)
12 Kalamata olives, pitted and halved

1. Preheat the oven to 300°F. Prepare a bain-marie (water bath) by putting a roasting pan or sheet pan on the center rack of the oven, filling it with about ½ inch of boiling water, and leaving it there while the oven preheats.

2. Grease 12 cups of a nonstick muffin tin with butter (if you don't have a nonstick muffin tin, be extra thorough with the butter).

3. Preheat a medium skillet over medium-high heat. When hot, swirl in the oil. Add the zucchini, bell pepper, scallions, chile flakes, and a few pinches of salt and pepper to taste. Cook just until the veggies soften, 4 to 6 minutes. Remove the pan from the heat, stir in the fresh herbs, and set aside.

4. In a blender, combine the eggs, cottage cheese, potato starch, and ¼ teaspoon salt and blend until completely smooth.

5. Divide the mixture among the prepared muffin cups, filling each one a little over the halfway mark. Dividing evenly, top with the sautéed veggies, feta, and olives and give each one a quick stir so the veggies and cheese are well distributed.

6. Carefully place the muffin tin directly into the water bath. Bake until the egg bites are set in the centers, 35 to 40 minutes.

7. Carefully remove the muffin tin from the water and let cool for 5 minutes on a wire rack, then run a thin spatula or knife around each one and unmold them. Cool for another 10 minutes before eating. Once cool, they'll keep for up to 4 days in an airtight container in the refrigerator or for a month in the freezer.

Change It Up

Easy swaps: Any cooked vegetable can be used as a filling, such as your favorite wilted greens, leftover roasted vegetables, sautéed mushrooms, or caramelized onions. Similarly, your favorite cheese can be substituted for the feta.

Amp it up: Sprinkle cooked, crumbled bacon or diced deli ham into the cups along with the vegetables.

CHOCOLATE CHIP & BANANA BREAKFAST COOKIES

Like a healthy bowl of oatmeal in cookie form, these are a favorite morning treat on busy days when we're rushing out the door. They're full of fiber-rich oats and healthy olive oil and have just enough sweetness from brown sugar and banana to pass the "cookie" test—which means that kids always love them. A spring-loaded cookie scoop makes portioning the dough extra easy.

Makes 18 cookies
Ready in 25 minutes

⅓ cup Greek olive oil
½ cup packed light brown sugar
1 large egg
1 teaspoon vanilla extract
1 small-to-medium ripe banana
¾ cup oat flour
½ teaspoon ground cinnamon
½ teaspoon baking soda
¼ teaspoon fine sea salt
½ cup rolled oats
⅔ cup semisweet chocolate chips

1. Preheat the oven to 350°F. Line a standard 18 by 13-inch baking sheet with parchment paper.

2. In a large bowl, whisk together the oil, brown sugar, egg, and vanilla. Add the banana and mash it into the mixture until well combined. Stir in the oat flour, cinnamon, baking soda, and salt. Fold in the oats and chocolate chips. Let the dough rest for 15 to 20 minutes to thicken up slightly.

3. Shape into 2-tablespoon portions of dough and space them out on the prepared baking sheet.

4. Transfer the pan to the oven and bake the cookies until the edges turn golden, 12 to 14 minutes.

5. Remove the pan from the oven and let the cookies cool on the pan for 5 to 10 minutes before eating. Packed in an airtight container, they'll keep for up to 3 days at room temperature or for 1 month in the freezer.

Change It Up

Easy swaps: Any neutral-tasting oil or melted butter can be substituted for the olive oil. Use your favorite nuts, seeds, or dried fruits in place of (or in addition to) the chocolate chips.

BABA'S GRAIN-FREE PANCAKES
with Easy Fruit Compote

This is one of the first recipes I ever shared on Hungry Happens, and it's very special to me because these were my baba's (my dad's) favorite pancakes. It wasn't often that he'd request I cook for him, since my yiayia and mom are such phenomenal cooks, but he liked these pancakes so much he asked for them often. Like me, Baba was fairly health minded about what he ate, always preferring homemade meals with recognizable ingredients over convenience foods, and he liked that these use whole ingredients and are light yet filling.

Serves 4
Ready in 15 minutes

2 cups superfine almond flour
1 teaspoon baking powder
2 teaspoons pumpkin pie spice or ground cinnamon
6 large eggs
½ cup canned sweet potato puree
2 tablespoons maple syrup or honey
2 tablespoons natural creamy nut butter (any kind)
1 teaspoon vanilla extract
Greek olive oil or butter, for greasing the pan (optional)
Easy Fruit Compote (recipe follows), for topping

Note: If you have leftover roasted sweet potatoes, you can use them for the canned puree here by peeling and pureeing them in a blender or mashing them thoroughly with a fork, then measuring out ½ cup of the mixture.

1. In a mixing bowl, stir together the almond flour, baking powder, pumpkin pie spice, eggs, sweet potato puree, maple syrup, nut butter, and vanilla and whisk until smooth.

2. Preheat a griddle or skillet over medium heat for about 5 minutes. If using a nonstick griddle, you won't need any fat for greasing; otherwise, add a little oil or butter and swirl the pan to coat it. Turn down the heat to medium-low.

3. Working in batches, ladle portions of batter onto the hot griddle, about 3 tablespoons each, giving them room to spread. Cook until darkened on the bottoms and bubbles appear on the tops, 2 to 3 minutes. Flip and cook until lightly browned and set in the centers, another 2 to 3 minutes.

4. Serve hot with warm fruit compote spooned over them. Cooked pancakes can be kept warm on a parchment-lined baking sheet in a preheated 250°F oven.

Change It Up

Easy swaps: Pumpkin or butternut squash puree or mashed bananas can be substituted for the sweet potato. Oat flour can be used in place of the almond flour.

EASY FRUIT COMPOTE
Makes about 1½ cups

2 teaspoons coconut oil
2 cups blueberries, raspberries, or strawberries, fresh or frozen
1 to 2 tablespoons maple syrup

In a small saucepan, melt the coconut oil over medium-low heat. Add the berries and maple syrup, bring to a simmer, and cook until the juices thicken slightly, 5 to 7 minutes. Serve warm.

COCOA DUTCH BABY
with Fresh Strawberries

A Dutch baby is a showstopper dish for brunch and special occasions. It puffs up dramatically in the oven and then deflates into a giant pancake with crispy edges and a custardy texture that forms a perfect vessel for your favorite fruit toppings. It also couldn't be easier to make. This chocolate Dutch baby itself isn't overly sweet because additional sweetness comes from the fresh strawberries, a big dollop of thick Greek yogurt, and chopped up dark chocolate, which melts into irresistible little puddles from the residual heat.

Serves 4
Ready in 30 minutes

- 3 large eggs, at room temperature
- ⅔ cup whole milk, at room temperature
- 2 tablespoons honey or maple syrup
- 1 teaspoon vanilla extract
- ⅓ cup all-purpose flour
- 3 tablespoons unsweetened cocoa powder
- ¼ teaspoon fine sea salt
- 3 tablespoons unsalted butter
- ¼ cup chopped semisweet chocolate or chocolate chips
- ½ cup quartered or sliced hulled strawberries
- Whole milk Greek yogurt, for serving
- Confectioners' sugar or maple syrup, for dusting or drizzling

1. Preheat the oven to 425°F. Place an ovenproof medium skillet (such as a 10-inch cast-iron one) in the oven during the preheat, for at least 10 minutes, so that it's thoroughly hot.

2. In a blender, combine the eggs, milk, honey, vanilla, flour, cocoa powder, and salt and process until completely smooth.

3. Carefully remove the skillet from the oven, using mitted hands, and add the butter, swirling it around to coat the sides and entire base. Pour in the batter.

4. Return the pan to the oven and bake the Dutch baby until the edges puff up the sides of the pan, 20 to 24 minutes.

5. Right out of the oven (it will deflate a bit), scatter the chocolate over the top, followed by the strawberries. Slide the Dutch baby onto a serving plate and cut it into quarters. Serve with dollops of yogurt and a little confectioners' sugar or maple syrup.

Change It Up

Easy swaps: Instead of strawberries, use a combination of blueberries and blackberries—or your favorite sliced or diced fruit.

Make it gluten-free: Use a gluten-free flour blend.

BAKED EGG TORTILLA
with Ham & Beans

FAN FAVORITE

This breakfast comes together entirely in a single baking dish and tastes like a cross between a quesadilla and a burrito. My favorite part is its assortment of textures—warm cheesy fillings in the center and crunchy baked tortilla edges that are perfect for scooping up any stray bits. Any large burrito-size tortilla works, including low-carb or high-protein options, and I encourage you to embrace the flexibility of the recipe, using whatever breakfast fillings you like best.

Serves 2
Ready in 20 minutes

Olive oil cooking spray, for greasing the baking dish
1 (10-inch) flour tortilla ("burrito-size")
2 large eggs
1 thin slice Black Forest ham, diced
¼ cup whole milk cottage cheese
¼ cup canned pinto or black beans, drained and rinsed
6 cherry tomatoes, halved
6 Kalamata olives, pitted and halved
¼ cup finely chopped green bell pepper (about ¼ pepper)
¼ cup finely diced red onion (about ¼ medium onion)
Fine sea salt and freshly ground black pepper
¼ cup shredded Cheddar cheese
Sriracha sauce, for garnish
Chopped chives or thinly sliced scallion, green and white part, for garnish

1. Preheat the oven to 400°F. Lightly spray a small baking dish (see Note) with the cooking spray.

2. Set the tortilla into the baking dish and gently press the edges up against its sides. Crack in the eggs. Scatter them evenly with the ham, dollops of cottage cheese, beans, tomatoes, olives, bell pepper, and onion. Season with a few pinches of salt and pepper. Finally, sprinkle the Cheddar over the top.

3. Transfer the baking dish to the oven and bake the tortilla until the whites of the eggs are set and the yolks are cooked to your liking—start checking after 15 minutes and then every minute or two, until they're as runny or firm as you please.

4. Remove the baking dish from the oven and carefully slide the tortilla onto a cutting board. Garnish with some sriracha and chives. Cut the tortilla in half, then to eat, fold it in half like a taco or gyro.

Note: I have a small ceramic baking dish that measures 10 by 7 inches that I use for this recipe, but any smaller baking vessel, such as a pie pan or a small ovenproof skillet, will work.

Change It Up
Make it vegetarian: Double the beans and omit the ham.

HOW TO QUICKLY LINE A PAN WITH PARCHMENT PAPER Trimming parchment to perfectly fit a loaf or cake pan can be so tedious. Here's my shortcut: Take a large piece of parchment, one big enough to cover the base and sides of the pan you need to line, scrunch it into a ball, then flatten it back out. It's now more malleable and easier to press into the corners of the pan.

BANANA-OAT BREAD
with Blueberries

Banana bread is often more like dessert than a healthy breakfast or snack, but mine uses nutrient-dense whole ingredients, like oats and frozen blueberries, that I always have on hand. And rather than granulated sugar, its sweetness comes primarily from the bananas. The batter gets blitzed up in seconds in the blender, so it's easy to make at a moment's notice. I love reheating the leftovers in the toaster oven and drizzling slices with tahini and a little honey.

Serves 8
Ready in 45 minutes

3 overripe medium bananas
2 large eggs
2 cups rolled oats
1 teaspoon vanilla extract
1 teaspoon baking soda
½ teaspoon ground cinnamon
Pinch of fine sea salt
¼ cup maple syrup or honey
½ cup blueberries, fresh or frozen (see Note)

1. Preheat the oven to 350°F. Line a 9 by 5-inch or 8 by 4-inch loaf pan with parchment paper (see my parchment-lining tip on page 40).

2. In a blender or food processor, combine the bananas, eggs, oats, vanilla, baking soda, cinnamon, salt, and maple syrup in that order and process until smooth. It will be a very liquid batter.

3. Pour the batter into the prepared loaf pan and scatter the blueberries on top.

4. Transfer the pan to the oven and bake until a toothpick tester comes out mostly clean (a few crumbs are fine), 35 to 40 minutes.

5. Remove the pan from the oven and allow the bread to cool in the pan for at least 20 minutes, then carefully remove the loaf from the pan and continue cooling for another 20 minutes before slicing. Wrapped loosely, it will keep for up to 3 days at room temperature or when stored in an airtight bag or container, for a month in the freezer.

Note: No need to thaw the blueberries if you're using frozen ones. Just add them to the batter straight from the freezer.

Change It Up

Easy swaps: Instead of (or in addition to) the blueberries, add ½ cup chocolate chips, ½ cup chopped walnuts, or ½ cup chopped dates or raisins.

If you don't have a blender: Mash up the bananas in a bowl, then whisk in the remaining ingredients, substituting 1 cup oat flour for the rolled oats.

VEGGIE QUICHE
in a Smashed Potato Crust

This is a fun, unique way to make a quiche crust: Just smash cooked potatoes into the pie pan! They take on a crisp-tender texture that perfectly holds the eggy filling. In addition, my custard incorporates cottage cheese, making it higher in protein and lighter than a traditional quiche, so it's a satisfying, feel-good entrée for a weekend brunch. It's also a great dish to make in advance, because it tastes good warm or at room temperature.

Serves 6
Ready in 1 hour 20 minutes

- 3 medium Yukon gold potatoes (12 ounces total), cut into 1- to 2-inch chunks
- Olive oil cooking spray, for greasing the pan and spraying the crust
- ¾ cup shredded Parmesan cheese, plus more for sprinkling
- Fine sea salt
- 1 tablespoon Greek olive oil, plus more for brushing
- ½ bell pepper (any color), cut into strips
- 1 cup cherry tomatoes, halved
- 2 cups baby spinach (2 ounces)
- 3 scallions, green and white parts, thinly sliced
- ¼ cup Kalamata olives, pitted and halved
- 4 large eggs
- ¾ cup whole milk cottage cheese
- ¼ cup heavy cream, half-and-half, or whole milk
- 1 teaspoon Italian seasoning
- Freshly ground black pepper
- 2 tablespoons chopped fresh parsley

1. Fill a pot or medium saucepan with 1 inch of water and fit with a steamer basket. Bring the water to a boil, then add the potatoes and cover. Steam the potatoes until tender and easily pierced with a paring knife, 14 to 17 minutes. Transfer them to a plate to cool until safe to handle, about 10 minutes.

2. Preheat the oven to 400°F. Spray a 9-inch pie pan, preferably a deep-dish one, with the cooking spray.

3. Sprinkle ½ cup of the Parmesan all over the bottom and sides of the prepared pan. Put the potatoes in the pan and use a flat-bottomed object (such as a measuring cup or shot glass) to smash them. Use your fingers to press the smashed potatoes into an even crust. Sprinkle the remaining ¼ cup Parmesan and a few pinches of salt over the crust and then spray it with the cooking spray.

4. Transfer the pan to the oven and bake until the crust is lightly browned, 20 to 25 minutes.

5. Meanwhile, preheat a medium skillet over medium-high heat until hot. Swirl in the oil. Add the bell pepper and sauté, stirring occasionally, until lightly caramelized, 3 to 5 minutes. Stir in the tomatoes and cook just until they start to soften, 3 to 5 minutes. Add the spinach and stir until it's just wilted. Remove the pan from the heat and stir in the scallions and olives.

6. In a small bowl, whisk together the eggs, cottage cheese, cream, Italian seasoning, ½ teaspoon salt, and pepper to taste.

7. Remove the crust from the oven but leave the oven on. Turn down the temperature to 325°F.

8. Spread the cooked vegetables evenly over the crust and slowly add the egg mixture. Return the pan to the oven and bake until the filling is set in the center, 32 to 35 minutes.

9. Remove the pan from the oven and let cool on a wire rack for at least 15 minutes before slicing.

10. Serve warm or at room temperature.

Change It Up

Easy swaps: Any cooked vegetables you like can be subbed in, such as kale, zucchini, mushrooms, or asparagus. You'll need a total of about 1½ cups of filling.

Amp it up: Add four slices of crumbled cooked bacon or up to 1 cup of diced deli ham along with the vegetable filling.

ELINA'S PUMPKIN-CHOCOLATE CHIP MUFFINS

This is a recipe I created many years ago, but I have my daughter, Elina, to thank for perfecting it. She makes these muffins all the time, sometimes twice a week! They have a super-soft texture that nobody can resist, and like all my baked goods, they're quick to whip up and easy to riff on. I like to reheat the leftovers in the toaster oven, splitting them open to tuck a bit of tahini or almond butter inside.

Makes 12 muffins
Ready in 35 minutes

Olive oil cooking spray, for greasing the muffin tin (optional)
⅓ cup Greek olive oil
½ cup maple syrup or honey
2 large eggs
1 cup canned pumpkin puree
¼ cup whole milk or nondairy milk
1 teaspoon ground cinnamon
1 teaspoon baking soda
1 teaspoon vanilla extract
½ teaspoon fine sea salt
⅛ teaspoon ground nutmeg
1¾ cups oat flour or all-purpose flour
½ cup semisweet chocolate chips, plus more for sprinkling (optional)

1. Preheat the oven to 325°F. Spray twelve cups of a muffin tin with the cooking spray or line with paper liners.

2. In a large bowl, whisk together the oil and maple syrup until smooth, then beat in the eggs until incorporated. Beat in the pumpkin, milk, cinnamon, baking soda, vanilla, salt, and nutmeg. Add the flour and stir just until combined. Fold in the chocolate chips.

3. Divide the batter among the muffin cups, filling each about three-quarters full. Top each muffin with a few more chocolate chips, if desired.

4. Transfer the muffin tin to the oven and bake the muffins until a toothpick tester comes out clean, 22 to 25 minutes.

5. Remove the muffin tin from the oven and let the muffins cool for 5 minutes in the tin, then unmold onto a wire rack to cool completely before eating. Packed in an airtight container, they'll keep for up to 3 days at room temperature or for 1 month in the freezer.

Change It Up

Easy swaps: Mix in walnuts, pecans, raisins, or chopped dates for some or all of the chocolate chips. Melted coconut oil, melted butter, or avocado oil can be used in place of olive oil. And pureed sweet potatoes or butternut squash can be used in place of the pumpkin.

BREAKFAST BISCUIT LOAF

This one-bowl savory loaf has breakfast sandwich vibes, with an aroma that's guaranteed to get everyone out of bed. It reminds me of the McDonald's breakfasts my brother and I would sometimes get on our way to high school. If you ever have such a craving, this easy homemade alternative will scratch the itch. The texture is rich, tender, and biscuitlike, and while it's hard to beat a drive-through for convenience, the recipe is extremely low effort. Leftovers are a treat, toasted and spread with cream cheese or with a sunny-side egg on top.

Serves 10
Ready in 55 minutes

- ¾ cup sour cream or whole milk Greek yogurt
- ⅓ cup Greek olive oil or melted unsalted butter
- 1 large egg
- 1 tablespoon maple syrup or honey
- 1½ cups all-purpose flour or oat flour
- 1 teaspoon baking powder
- ½ teaspoon baking soda
- ½ teaspoon fine sea salt
- 1½ cups shredded sharp Cheddar cheese
- 6 slices bacon, cooked (see page 184) and chopped or crumbled
- 2 tablespoons minced fresh chives

1. Preheat the oven to 350°F. Line a 9 by 5-inch or 8 by 4-inch loaf pan with parchment paper (see my parchment-lining tip on page 40).

2. In a large bowl, whisk together the sour cream, oil, egg, and maple syrup until combined. Sift in the flour, baking powder, baking soda, and salt and stir gently until just combined. Fold in the Cheddar, bacon, and chives. The batter will be very thick.

3. Scrape the batter into the prepared pan and compress it into a smooth, even thickness.

4. Transfer the pan to the oven and bake the bread until a toothpick tester comes out clean, 40 to 45 minutes.

5. Remove the pan from the oven and let the bread cool in the pan for 10 minutes, then unmold and cool completely on a wire rack before slicing. Packed in an airtight container, it will keep for up to 3 days at room temperature or for 1 month in the freezer.

Note: While both sizes of loaf pan work for this recipe, a smaller 8 by 4-inch pan will yield a slightly taller loaf.

Change It Up

Easy swaps: Use another sharp cheese, such as Gruyère, Gouda, or pepper jack in place of Cheddar. Diced deli ham can be substituted for the bacon.

SUNSET MEZZE

2

When I'm in Greece every summer, mezze hour is my most favorite part of the day. The sun is setting over the water, the temperature has cooled ever so slightly, and everyone wanders outdoors to the local restaurants to congregate around delicious little bites that whet the appetite for the evening to come. I'll often even make the whole dinner about the mezze, skipping the entrées altogether! Collected here are the showstopper appetizers I make most often at home, featuring classic Greek flavors as well as some of my most popular Hungry Happens recipes. They're a perfect way to kick off a dinner party—even if they end up being the dinner itself.

GARIDOPETOULES
Shrimp Fritters

These rich, cheesy crab cake–like fritters hail from Monemvasia, Greece, which is the area where my family is from. Traditionally, they're made from tiny shrimp that are native to the area and deep-fried. But over the years, I've adapted the recipe to use standard wild shrimp and lightened things up by pan-frying them in a nonstick skillet. I typically prefer my cooked appetizers warm, but you can serve these fritters at room temperature or even straight from the fridge and they're absolutely delicious.

Makes 12 fritters
Ready in 1½ hours

- 1 pound peeled and deveined wild shrimp, cut into ½-inch pieces
- 1 teaspoon paprika or Old Bay seasoning
- Fine sea salt
- 2 large eggs
- ¼ cup mayonnaise or whole milk Greek yogurt
- ¼ cup potato starch or all-purpose flour
- 4 ounces Greek feta cheese, crumbled (about 1 cup)
- ½ cup shredded mozzarella cheese
- ¼ cup finely chopped red bell pepper
- 2 scallions, green and white parts, thinly sliced
- 3 tablespoons chopped fresh dill
- 1 tablespoon fresh lemon juice (½ medium lemon)
- Freshly ground black pepper
- 2 tablespoons Greek olive oil plus more, for frying
- Chopped fresh dill, for garnish
- Lemon wedges, for squeezing
- Lazy Tzatziki (page 200), for serving

1. Season the shrimp pieces all over with paprika and a few pinches of salt.

2. In a large bowl, whisk together the eggs and mayo. Stir in the potato starch, feta, mozzarella, bell pepper, scallions, 3 tablespoons dill, lemon juice, ½ teaspoon salt, and pepper to taste. Fold in the shrimp and mix to combine. Cover and refrigerate for 1 hour.

3. Line a plate with paper towels and place near the stove. Preheat a wide skillet over medium-high heat until hot. Swirl in 2 tablespoons oil. Scoop the batter into the pan in scant ⅓-cup portions, adding as many as will fit without crowding, so they're easy to flip. Cook until golden brown on both sides, 3 to 4 minutes per side. Transfer the cooked fritters to the paper towels to drain. Wipe out the pan, add fresh oil, and repeat with the remaining batter.

4. Serve hot, garnished with dill. Serve lemon wedges and tzatziki on the side.

SESAME-CRUSTED BAKED FETA
with Hot Honey

In Greek cuisine, cheese features in nearly every part of the meal, starting with the mezze, and I especially love warm cheese dishes such as fried saganaki or baked feta me meli (feta with honey). This recipe is suitable for last-minute needs because unlike those classic dishes, you don't need to thaw a whole package of phyllo. Instead, feta is dredged in seedy, spiced panko bread crumbs that form a crunchy crust, which contrasts with the soft, warm, salty cheese. Then it's finished with a generous drizzle of hot honey, making it impossible to resist.

Serves 4 to 6
Ready in 35 minutes

¼ cup panko bread crumbs
2 tablespoons sesame seeds
¼ teaspoon onion powder
¼ teaspoon fine sea salt
¼ teaspoon Italian seasoning
1 large egg
2 tablespoons all-purpose flour
1 (7- to 8-ounce) block Greek feta cheese
Hot honey, for drizzling
Crackers or sliced baguette, for serving

1. Preheat the oven to 400°F. Line a small baking dish or ovenproof skillet with parchment paper.

2. In a shallow bowl or plate, stir together the panko, sesame seeds, onion powder, salt, and Italian seasoning. Place the egg in a separate shallow plate or bowl and whisk it until evenly combined.

3. Sprinkle the flour all over the feta, dredge it in the beaten egg, then coat all the sides in the panko-sesame mixture, gently pressing so the panko adheres. Set the crusted cheese in the prepared baking dish.

4. Transfer the dish to the oven and bake until golden brown all over, 20 to 25 minutes. If you'd like to get darker browning on the crust, switch the oven to broil and place the feta beneath the heat source for 1 to 3 minutes, watching carefully.

5. Remove the pan from the oven and drizzle the cheese with hot honey.

6. Serve immediately with the crackers.

Change It Up
Easy swaps: A round of Boursin cheese is a great substitute for the feta.

BALSAMIC ROASTED STRAWBERRIES
with Whipped Honey-Ricotta

This simple recipe employs two tricks worth committing to memory. First is the whipped ricotta, which only requires blending the fresh cheese in a food processor to transform it into a soft and silky, decadent cream. The second trick is roasting strawberries with a bit of balsamic vinegar; this imparts a complex, deep, jammy flavor to the fruit, turning it into something of a compote. It pairs beautifully with the cheese and makes for an unexpected, sweet-savory option to add to the usual spread of snacks (and it makes a very nice light dessert, too).

Serves 4 to 6
Ready in 40 minutes

Roasted Strawberries
1 pound strawberries, hulled and halved (or quartered if large)
2 tablespoons honey
1 tablespoon balsamic vinegar
1 tablespoon Greek olive oil
Pinch of fine sea salt

Whipped Honey-Ricotta
1½ cups good-quality ricotta cheese
1½ to 3 tablespoons honey

Balsamic vinegar, for drizzling
Honey, for drizzling
Fresh mint leaves, for garnish
Crackers or toasts, for serving

1. To roast the strawberries: Preheat the oven to 425°F. Line a standard 18 by 13-inch baking sheet with parchment paper.

2. In a bowl, combine the berries, honey, vinegar, oil, and salt and toss well to evenly coat. Scrape the contents of the bowl onto the prepared pan.

3. Transfer the pan to the oven and bake until the juices thicken and the berries are tender, 18 to 22 minutes, stirring every 10 minutes.

4. Remove the pan from the oven and allow to cool for at least 10 minutes. (The strawberries can be made up to a day in advance and stored in an airtight container in the refrigerator. Bring to room temperature before serving.)

5. To make the honey-ricotta: In a food processor, blend the ricotta and 1½ tablespoons honey until light and smooth. Taste, adding more honey if desired. (The ricotta can also be made up to a day in advance and stored in an airtight container in the refrigerator.)

6. When ready to serve: Smear the whipped ricotta over a serving bowl and top with the roasted strawberries, which can be warm or at room temperature. Drizzle with a bit more vinegar and honey and garnish with the mint. Serve with the crackers.

MELITZANOSALATA GARLIC BREAD
Cheesy Garlic Bread Topped with Greek Eggplant Dip

Similar to baba ghanoush, melitzanosalata is a Greek dip made from roasted eggplant. There are many variations around Greece, but typically it's quite light, lemony, and pungent with fresh garlic. It makes a great dip for flatbreads or toasts, but I like to give it this garlic bread treatment, smearing it over a loaf of crusty, buttery garlic bread that's capped with cheese and broiled until everything is hot and melty. It's great as a snack or appetizer but equally delicious as a side dish, particularly with a big summery menu of grilled meats and fresh salads.

Serves 8
Ready in 1½ hours

 VT

Melitzanosalata (Eggplant Dip)
2 medium eggplants (2 pounds total)
¼ cup Greek olive oil, plus more for greasing the eggplants
1 garlic clove, minced
1 tablespoon fresh lemon juice (½ medium lemon)
½ teaspoon fine sea salt
Freshly ground black pepper

Garlic Bread
1 large loaf Italian bread, such as ciabatta
4 tablespoons unsalted butter, melted
2 garlic cloves, minced
2 tablespoons minced fresh parsley
Fine sea salt
1 (8-ounce) ball mozzarella cheese, thinly sliced, or 2 cups shredded Gouda or fontina cheese
Chopped fresh parsley, for garnish
Red chile flakes, for garnish

Note: The melitzanosalata can be made up to a day in advance.

1. To make the dip: Preheat the oven to 425°F. Line a baking sheet with parchment paper.

2. Halve the eggplants lengthwise through the stem and rub a little oil over the cut sides. Place them cut-side down on the pan.

3. Transfer the pan to the oven and roast the eggplants until fork-tender, 30 to 40 minutes.

4. Remove the pan from the oven but leave the oven on. Allow the eggplants to cool until safe to handle, then use a spoon to scoop the flesh off the skin and transfer the flesh to a colander to drain. Discard the skin.

5. Coarsely mash the eggplant. Add the oil, garlic, lemon juice, salt, and pepper to taste. Taste and adjust the seasoning as needed.

6. To prepare the garlic bread: Line a baking sheet with parchment paper.

7. Slice the bread in half horizontally and arrange it cut-side up on the prepared pan. In a small bowl, stir together the butter, garlic, parsley, and a pinch of salt. Brush the mixture evenly all over the cut sides of the bread.

8. Transfer the pan to the oven and bake the bread until it starts to brown around the edges, 7 to 10 minutes.

9. Remove the pan from the oven and the bread top with the eggplant dip, dividing it between the two pieces and spreading it evenly. Arrange the cheese on top.

10. Return the pan to the oven and bake until the cheese is melted and the eggplant dip is heated through, 7 to 10 minutes more. To get some browning on the cheese, switch the oven to broil and place the pan beneath the heat source for 1 to 3 minutes, watching carefully.

11. Remove the pan from the oven and garnish the bread with the parsley and a few pinches of chile flakes.

12. Serve warm, sliced into pieces.

DINER CHEESEBURGER BITES
with Special Sauce

Growing up in the restaurant business, a cheeseburger with fries was my go-to order at my father's diner. The smell of the two foods will forever remind me of working there, evoking so many memories, and to this day, I still love a cheeseburger—especially right when I get back from Greece every summer. This recipe is an homage to our family diner's most popular order. I've refashioned it into a three-bite appetizer that's baked in a muffin tin, where the beef "patty" is crusted in cheese. There's no bun involved, making these a great low-carb snack, but I encourage you to dress them up with all your favorite burger toppings!

Makes 16 bites
Ready in 1 hour

Cheeseburger Bites
1 pound ground beef (95/5)
¾ teaspoon fine sea salt
½ teaspoon onion powder
½ teaspoon garlic powder
½ teaspoon paprika
4 cups shredded Mexican cheese blend (1 pound)
4 slices bacon, cooked (see page 184) and crumbled or chopped
¼ sweet onion, finely diced
16 round pickle slices
Toasted sesame seeds for garnish (optional)

Special Sauce
½ cup mayonnaise
2 tablespoons ketchup
2 tablespoons white wine vinegar
2 tablespoons chopped pickles or relish
1 tablespoon yellow mustard
1 tablespoon finely diced sweet onion
1 teaspoon honey
½ teaspoon paprika
¼ teaspoon garlic powder
¼ teaspoon onion powder
¼ teaspoon fine sea salt

1. To make the cheeseburger bites: Preheat the oven to 375°F.

2. Preheat a wide skillet over medium-high heat until hot. Add the ground beef and cook, using a wooden spoon to break up the meat into crumbles, until it's no longer pink, 5 to 7 minutes. Season with the salt, onion powder, garlic powder, and paprika.

3. Add a generous 1½ tablespoons shredded cheese to sixteen cups of two standard muffin tins, pushing the cheese into the bottoms and up the sides to form a crust. Divide the beef among the cups, about 2 tablespoons each. Dividing evenly, top each with a sprinkle of bacon, some diced onion, and a pickle slice. Top each with another 1½ tablespoons shredded cheese, dividing the rest of it over the cups.

4. Transfer the muffin tins to the oven and bake the bites until the cheese has melted and the edges of each cup are crispy, 13 to 15 minutes.

5. Remove the muffin tin from the oven and let the bites rest in the pan for 10 minutes so the cheese can firm up slightly, then use a thin spatula to pop each one out. Garnish with the sesame seeds if desired.

6. To make the sauce: In a bowl, whisk together all the ingredients until smooth. Taste and adjust the seasoning as needed.

7. Serve the hot or warm cheeseburger bites with the sauce on the side as a dip or spooned on top.

Note: While Cheddar or any nicely melting cheese will work here, a Mexi-blend cheese is best because it releases less oil as it melts.

AIR-FRYER ARTICHOKE BITES
with Aioli

Crispy, breaded artichoke hearts aren't nearly as popular as they should be. Their uniquely sweet flavor and creamy texture, tucked inside a savory, crispy crust, is so unexpectedly delicious—and if you aren't convinced, these two-bite treats will provide proof. The air fryer works wonders to ensure golden crispiness all around and also makes it easy to cook them in batches since they're best served while still hot. And don't be intimidated by making the aioli. With the food processor, it's practically foolproof.

Serves 6 to 8
Ready in 30 minutes

1 (14- to 16-ounce) jar whole artichoke hearts in brine or water, drained
¼ cup all-purpose flour
1 large egg
2 tablespoons water
1 cup panko bread crumbs
1 tablespoon Greek olive oil
¾ teaspoon fine sea salt
½ teaspoon garlic powder
½ teaspoon onion powder
½ teaspoon Italian seasoning
Freshly ground black pepper
Aioli (recipe follows)

1. Cut each artichoke heart in half through the stem. Spread them out on a few layers of paper towels and gently blot them dry.

2. Set up a dredging station in three bowls: Put the flour in one bowl. Crack the egg into a second bowl and whisk it with the water until well combined. In the third bowl, stir together the panko, oil, salt, garlic powder, onion powder, Italian seasoning, and a few grinds of pepper, incorporating the oil well so the mixture doesn't clump.

3. Preheat an air fryer to 375°F. (See Change It Up below for using a traditional oven.)

4. Working with a few pieces at a time, dredge the artichoke halves first through the flour, then dip in the egg mixture, and roll in the panko. Working in batches if necessary, arrange the breaded artichokes in the air-fryer pan or basket in a single layer, spacing them out by about ½ inch.

5. Air-fry until golden brown and crispy, 6 to 8 minutes, flipping them once halfway through.

6. Serve hot with the aioli on the side for dipping.

AIOLI
Makes 1¼ cups

½ cup Greek olive oil
½ cup avocado oil
1 large egg
1 teaspoon Dijon mustard
1 garlic clove, finely grated
2 tablespoons fresh lemon juice (1 medium lemon)
Fine sea salt

1. In a measuring cup with a spout, combine the two oils.

2. In a food processor or mini food processor, blend together the egg, mustard, and garlic until combined. With the motor running, start adding the oil just a few drops at a time, letting it blend into the egg before each new addition. Continue adding the rest of the oil *very* slowly, making sure the oil blends into the egg each time before adding more, periodically stopping to scrape down the sides of the food processor bowl.

3. With the motor running, add the lemon juice and then blend in ¼ teaspoon salt. Taste and adjust the seasoning as needed. The aioli will keep in an airtight container in the refrigerator for up to 1 week.

Change It Up

Baked Artichoke Bites: Preheat the oven to 400°F. Arrange the breaded artichokes in a single layer on a parchment-lined baking sheet. Bake until the crust is golden and crispy, 10 to 15 minutes, flipping them halfway through.

A NOTE ON PARMESAN When I list Parmesan cheese in a recipe, it'll be in one of three ways: When I say "grated," I mean finely grated, to an almost powdery texture. "Shredded" Parmesan is a little coarser, fashioned into small strands of the cheese. In both these instances, pre-grated/shredded cheese will work fine and can be a helpful way to save some time. But when I call for "freshly grated" Parmesan, it should be shaved from a wedge, using a rasp-style grater like a Microplane. Additionally, Pecorino Romano is an easy substitute for Parmesan in any of my recipes. Lastly, if you are a strict vegetarian, look for vegetarian Parmesan cheese that lists "microbial rennet" as an ingredient, since traditional Parmesan uses animal rennet.

SMASHED BROCCOLI CHIPS
with Spicy Ranch Dip

If you want your kids to eat more broccoli, these cheesy broccoli "chips"—one of my most popular viral recipes—are the answer! A week seldom goes by when I'm not asked to make them, and the method is so fun and simple, kids enjoy making them, too. Blanched broccoli is "smashed" into a bed of cheese, which then gets baked into a big, golden-crispy sheet that you'll break into shards. They're good enough to eat unadorned, but for me the spicy ranch dip is essential for dipping.

Serves 4
Ready in 45 minutes

Spicy Ranch Dip
½ cup mayonnaise
¼ cup buttermilk
2 tablespoons chopped fresh chives
1 tablespoon sriracha sauce
1 tablespoon rice vinegar
½ teaspoon onion powder
½ teaspoon garlic powder
Pinch of cayenne pepper (optional)

Broccoli Chips
Fine sea salt
3 broccoli crowns, trimmed into large florets
2½ cups shredded Parmesan cheese (10 ounces)
A few pinches of onion powder
A few pinches of garlic powder

1. To make the dip: In a small bowl, whisk together all the ingredients. Taste and adjust the seasoning as needed.

2. To make the chips: Preheat the oven to 400°F. Line a standard 18 by 13-inch baking sheet with parchment paper.

3. Line a platter with paper towels and place near the stove. Bring a pot of salted water to a boil. Add the broccoli and cook until the florets are just fork-tender, 1 to 2 minutes from when the water comes back to a boil, taking care not to overcook them. Drain and spread the broccoli out on the paper towels. Gently blot the broccoli dry.

4. Sprinkle the Parmesan over the prepared pan in a thin, even layer. Arrange the broccoli on top of the cheese, spacing out the florets. Using a small flat-bottomed object, such as a shot glass or measuring cup, smash each broccoli piece gently but firmly. Sprinkle all over with pinches of salt, onion powder, garlic powder, and cayenne (if using).

5. Transfer the pan to the oven and bake until the cheese has turned golden brown and the broccoli is beginning to crisp, 25 to 30 minutes.

6. Remove the pan from the oven and allow to cool slightly. Then using the parchment paper, carefully slide the whole unit onto a cutting board. While the cheese is still warm and pliable, peel off the parchment. Allow to cool completely, then break into bite-size chips and serve with the dip.

Change It Up

Easy swaps: This method works great with all kinds of other vegetables, such as Brussels sprouts, mushrooms, carrots, and potatoes or even apples. The parboiling time may be different, though, so watch closely, removing them from the water as soon as they're just fork-tender.

Note: Be sure to use large pieces of broccoli to create proper chips, taking care not to overcook them in the first blanching step.

BAKED HALLOUMI & GOUDA
in Puff Pastry

Halloumi is known for holding its shape throughout cooking, so while it's soft when hot, it doesn't necessarily melt. That's why I like to pair it with Gouda in this little puff pastry–wrapped parcel, both for its pronounced flavor but also to create meltiness inside. More important, the two cheeses blend gorgeously together as far as flavor goes. Choose an all-butter puff pastry if you can, and then serve this with an appetizer knife so that eaters can break into it.

Serves 8
Ready in 35 minutes

All-purpose flour, for dusting
1 sheet frozen puff pastry, thawed overnight in the refrigerator
1 (8- to 9-ounce) package Halloumi cheese, cut into ½-inch chunks
1 (8- to 9-ounce) wedge Gouda cheese, wax removed, cut into ½-inch chunks
1 tablespoon Greek olive oil
2 or 3 garlic cloves, finely minced
1 teaspoon dried oregano
1 teaspoon red chile flakes
1 egg, beaten with 1 tablespoon tap water, for the egg wash
Runny honey, for drizzling

1. Preheat the oven to 425°F. Line a medium baking dish, such as a 2-quart one or an ovenproof skillet, with parchment paper.

2. Dust a work surface lightly with flour and roll out the puff pastry into a 12- to 14-inch square (see Note). Arrange the cheese cubes in a single layer in the center. Drizzle the oil over the cheese and sprinkle evenly with the garlic, oregano, and chile flakes. Fold the puff pastry over the cheese so that it's wrapped up inside, pleating with a decorative seam or edge if you please. Place the parcel in the prepared pan. (At this point, you can cover the pan with plastic wrap and keep it in the refrigerator for up to a day.) When ready to bake, brush the outside of the pastry with the egg wash.

3. Transfer the pan to the oven and bake until the crust is deeply golden brown, 30 to 35 minutes.

4. Remove the pan from the oven and allow the cheese to cool for about 5 minutes, then drizzle all over with the honey.

5. Serve with cheese knives or spoons for guests to dig into at the table or cut into wedges or squares beforehand for easier serving.

Note: Different brands of puff pastry come in different sizes of sheets, but know that this is a very flexible recipe and any kind you use will work great. You can always roll out the pastry a little thinner if you've got a small sheet or leave it thick and fold the pastry around the cheese like a rustic tart, with some of the cheese exposed.

Change It Up

Add jam: Spoon ¼ to ½ cup fig jam (or any jam you like) evenly over the cheese and omit the honey at the end.

Swap the cheeses: Substitute feta for the halloumi, and/or mozzarella for the gouda.

CRISPY FETA-STUFFED OLIVES

Applying heat to good olives really transforms them into something new, softening both the flesh and the flavor. These olives are stuffed with feta and coated in crunchy bread crumbs. Traditionally, they're fried, but I lighten them up by cooking them in my oven or air fryer. They're absolutely irresistible at a cocktail party, when offered up warm and freshly baked. They work best with the largest pitted olives you can find (see my suggestions below), which make them easier to stuff with cheese. But if you'd like to speed up the process, purchase olives that have already been stuffed—with cheese, peppers, garlic, almonds, or anything you like.

Serves 6 to 8
Ready in 25 minutes

- 1 (10- to 12-ounce) jar large pitted green olives, such as gordal, Castelvetrano, or Cerignola, drained
- 1 ounce Greek feta cheese, crumbled (about ¼ cup)
- 2 tablespoons all-purpose flour or tapioca starch
- 1 large egg
- ½ cup fine dried bread crumbs
- ¼ cup grated Parmesan cheese
- ¼ teaspoon garlic powder
- 1 tablespoon Greek olive oil
- Freshly ground black pepper

1. Preheat the oven to 375°F or an air fryer to 350°F. Line a small baking sheet with parchment paper.

2. Blot the olives dry with paper towels. Working one at a time, stuff a few crumbles of feta cheese into each cavity.

3. Set up a dredging station in three shallow bowls: Put the flour in the first bowl. Crack the egg into the second bowl and whisk it until evenly combined. In the third bowl, mix together the bread crumbs, Parmesan, garlic powder, oil, and a few grinds of pepper to taste.

4. Working a few at a time, toss the olives through the flour, dip them in the egg, then roll them through the bread crumbs, making sure they're evenly coated at each stage. Arrange them on the prepared pan, spacing them out a little.

5. Bake or air-fry the olives until golden brown, 14 to 16 minutes. Cool for a few minutes, then serve while warm.

Change It Up
Swap the cheese: Use Boursin or goat cheese instead of the feta.

TAHINI-CRUSTED CHICKPEAS

Tahini takes these roasted chickpeas to the next level, creating a crunchy, spiced, and nutty shell for each individual bean. Since the recipe is so short and simple, you'll find dozens of ways to enjoy them as a snack to nibble on out of hand or as a garnish for salads and soups, like a healthy crouton. Their crunchiness hinges on getting the chickpeas as dry as possible, so be sure to blot them well to soak up as much excess moisture as you can.

Makes about 2 cups
Ready in 30 minutes

1 (15-ounce) can chickpeas, drained and rinsed
¼ cup well-stirred tahini
1 tablespoon black or white sesame seeds
½ teaspoon paprika
½ teaspoon onion powder
½ teaspoon fine sea salt

1. Preheat the oven to 400°F. Line a standard 18 by 13-inch baking sheet with parchment paper.

2. Spread the chickpeas out on a double layer of paper towels and roll them around a bit so they're as dry as possible. Transfer them to the prepared pan.

3. Transfer the pan to the oven for about 5 minutes to help them dry out further.

4. Meanwhile, in a bowl, whisk together the tahini, sesame seeds, paprika, onion powder, and salt until smooth.

5. Add the chickpeas to the bowl and toss to coat. Return them to the baking sheet and space them out so that none are touching.

6. Return the pan to the oven and bake until golden and crunchy, 24 to 28 minutes.

7. Remove the pan from the oven and let cool completely in the pan. Stored in an airtight container, the chickpeas will keep for 2 or 3 days at room temperature.

Change It Up
Easy swaps: Use your favorite nut or seed butter in place of the tahini.

SPINACH & FETA COOKIES

A little crunchy on the outside, pillowy soft on the inside, and absolutely bursting with classic Greek flavors, guests often start out being skeptical of these savory "cookies" when I serve them. But guess what? They disappear instantly! This is an extremely popular recipe of mine, not only for being unique and unforgettable but also because the batter comes together in minutes using just one bowl. It's a perfect party option when you want to offer a freshly baked treat but are short on time.

Makes 15 cookies
Ready in 35 minutes

1 large egg
¼ cup Greek olive oil or melted unsalted butter
¼ cup whole milk Greek yogurt
1½ cups chopped baby spinach (1½ ounces)
4 ounces feta cheese, crumbled (about 1 cup)
⅓ cup shredded mozzarella cheese
1 tablespoon chopped fresh dill
1 tablespoon chopped scallions (white parts only)
Pinch of fine sea salt
Freshly ground black pepper
1 cup self-rising flour, homemade (recipe follows) or store-bought

1. Preheat the oven to 350°F. Line a standard 18 by 13-inch baking sheet with parchment paper.

2. In a large bowl, whisk together the egg, oil, and yogurt until smooth. Stir in the spinach, feta, mozzarella, dill, scallions, salt, and a few grinds of pepper. Sift the flour over the mixture and stir it in. It will look dry at first but will eventually moisten up; you can use your hands if necessary. Shape the mixture into fifteen balls and arrange them on the prepared pan, pressing each one down slightly.

3. Transfer the pan to the oven and bake until golden brown, 17 to 20 minutes.

4. Remove the pan from the oven and allow the cookies to cool for at least 10 minutes before eating. Packed in an airtight container, they'll keep for up to 3 days at room temperature or for 1 month in the freezer.

HOMEMADE SELF-RISING FLOUR
Makes 1 cup

1 cup all-purpose flour
1 teaspoon baking powder
½ teaspoon fine sea salt
¼ teaspoon baking soda

In a small bowl, whisk together all the ingredients. Store in an airtight container at room temperature for up to 3 months.

SPICY SALMON-RICE MUFFINS

Think of these muffins as individual sushi roll cups, where all the bold flavors and delicious textures of a sushi roll are combined in a healthy snack that's easy to make and exciting to eat. It's one of my most popular recipes of all time, and for me it's also an affordable way to have "sushi night" at home, compared to what it costs to take everyone out to a restaurant. They're so flexible, too—customize them with your favorite sushi components by making the nori-rice cups and filling them with whatever you please.

Makes 12 muffins
Ready in 1 hour, not including marinating time

Marinated Salmon
1 pound wild salmon, skin removed, and cut into ¾-inch cubes
2 tablespoons sesame oil (not toasted) or Greek olive oil
1 tablespoon tamari or reduced-sodium soy sauce
1 tablespoon honey
2 scallions, green and white parts, thinly sliced
½ teaspoon garlic powder
½ teaspoon onion powder
½ teaspoon chili powder
½ teaspoon paprika
½ teaspoon dried oregano
A few pinches of fine sea salt

Spicy Mayo
¼ cup mayonnaise, preferably Kewpie
2 teaspoons sriracha sauce
1 teaspoon honey

Assembly
3 sheets nori
1½ cups cooked sushi rice, cooled
½ avocado, finely diced
2 teaspoons black or white sesame seeds

1. To marinate the salmon: In a medium bowl, combine all the ingredients and stir gently until evenly coated. Marinate for at least 30 minutes or up to 4 hours.

2. To make the mayo: Whisk together the mayo, sriracha, and honey until smooth.

3. When ready to assemble: Preheat the oven to 400°F.

4. Using scissors, cut each nori sheet into four evenly sized squares. Working with one square at a time, scoop 2 tablespoons of the cooked rice on top of each nori square. Use moistened hands to flatten it out into a thin, even round that covers most of the nori. Gently press the rice-covered square into a muffin cup, molding it against the shape of the pan so there's a cavity in the center. Repeat with the remaining nori and rice, filling up 12 cups of a standard muffin tin. Divide the salmon mixture among the cups, 4 or 5 pieces for each one.

5. Transfer the pan to the oven and bake until the salmon is cooked, 15 to 17 minutes. If you'd like to get some blistering on the salmon, switch the oven to broil and place it under the heat source for 1 to 2 minutes, watching carefully.

6. Remove the pan from the oven and allow to cool for about 5 minutes, then divide the avocado, sesame seeds, and mayo over the tops. Serve warm or at room temperature.

Change It Up

Spicy Shrimp-Rice Muffins: Substitute 1 pound peeled and deveined shrimp, cut into ¾-inch pieces, for the salmon.

3

HUNGRY IN A HURRY

I work hard to create speedy recipes, because no matter how much anybody enjoys cooking, less time spent in the kitchen is more time spent with loved ones or doing something more important. The recipes in this chapter tick all the boxes of being full of flavor, quick, and easy, mostly coming together in 30 minutes or less, and employing simple techniques that keep things low stress. And as always, I steer clear of store-bought ultraprocessed foods as shortcuts, instead making the most of good-quality, whole ingredients for maximum nutrition and flavor.

CHICKEN SAGANAKI

In Greek, "saganaki" translates simply to "little frying pan," and you probably know one of the most famous versions of the dish that features shrimp. I love to make it using chicken, too; this turns it into something different but equally good, with that classic mix of sweet heat and pops of saltiness from olives and soft, creamy feta. I think of it as a pantry dinner, because it relies primarily on jarred ingredients and standard spices; to that end, if you don't have roasted red peppers, use crushed tomatoes instead. Serve this with plain orzo or rice or for an extra-special pairing, with Lemony Orzotto (page 145).

Serves 4
Ready in 30 minutes

1½ pounds boneless, skinless chicken thighs, patted dry and cut in half
3 tablespoons Greek olive oil
1½ teaspoons fine sea salt
½ teaspoon paprika
½ teaspoon onion powder
½ teaspoon garlic powder
1 (16-ounce) jar roasted red peppers, drained
1 large shallot, finely minced
4 garlic cloves, minced
½ teaspoon red chile flakes
2 tablespoons tomato paste
¼ cup ouzo or ½ cup white wine
1 (14.5-ounce) can diced tomatoes, preferably fire-roasted
2 tablespoons dried oregano
1 tablespoon honey
Freshly ground black pepper
1 (7- to 8-ounce) block Greek feta cheese, cut into large cubes
⅓ cup pitted Kalamata olives, halved
2 tablespoons chopped fresh parsley
Crusty bread or cooked rice, for serving

1. Preheat the oven to 400°F.

2. In a bowl, combine the chicken, 2 tablespoons of the oil, 1 teaspoon of the salt, the paprika, onion powder, and garlic powder and toss until evenly coated.

3. Preheat a large ovenproof skillet over medium-high heat until hot. Add the chicken pieces in a single layer and sear each side until golden, 2 to 3 minutes per side. (You may need to work in batches.) Transfer the chicken to a plate or platter and cover with aluminum foil to keep it warm.

4. Meanwhile, in a countertop blender (or using an immersion blender), puree the roasted red peppers until smooth.

5. Turn down the heat under the skillet to medium. Add the remaining 1 tablespoon oil and the shallot and sauté until soft and translucent, 2 to 3 minutes. Stir in the garlic, chile flakes, and tomato paste and stir until coated, then add the ouzo. Add the diced tomatoes, roasted pepper puree, oregano, honey, the remaining ½ teaspoon salt, and pepper to taste. Bring to a boil. Turn down the heat to a simmer, partially cover, and cook until only slightly reduced, stirring occasionally, about 5 minutes. Taste the sauce and adjust the seasoning as needed, but keep in mind that feta and olives will be added, so be careful not to oversalt it.

6. Add the chicken to the sauce and nestle the feta pieces and olives in between.

7. Transfer the pan to the oven and bake until the chicken is cooked through, 8 to 10 minutes.

8. Remove the pan from the oven and sprinkle with the parsley.

9. Serve with crusty bread for dipping or on top of rice with lots of the sauce.

EASY LEMON-GARLIC-PARMESAN CHICKEN

This simple chicken recipe is super popular on Hungry Happens, because it effortlessly transforms a dish of baked chicken thighs into an absolutely unforgettable dinner. Parmesan cheese adds some extra oomph to the marinade, and by reserving a portion of it, the marinade doubles as a finishing sauce to spoon over the cooked meat, too. It's a great trick for adding an extra flavor boost and so much juiciness. Pair the chicken with a quick salad and some flatbreads, and dinner is complete.

Serves 6
Ready in 30 minutes, not including marinating time

2 pounds boneless, skinless chicken thighs, patted dry
¼ cup Greek olive oil
2 tablespoons fresh lemon juice (1 medium lemon)
1 tablespoon honey
4 garlic cloves, minced
1½ teaspoons fine sea salt
1 teaspoon paprika
1 teaspoon onion powder
½ teaspoon dried oregano
¼ teaspoon red chile flakes
Freshly ground black pepper
¼ cup grated Parmesan cheese

1. Place the chicken in a resealable plastic bag. In a small bowl or measuring glass, whisk together the oil, lemon juice, honey, garlic, salt, paprika, onion powder, oregano, chile flakes, and pepper to taste. Stir in the Parmesan. Add about three-quarters of the marinade to the chicken. Seal the bag, pressing out as much air as possible, and use your hands to stir the chicken so that it's evenly coated. Refrigerate for at least 30 minutes or up to overnight. Store the remaining portion of the marinade in a small airtight container in the refrigerator, keeping it from coming into contact with the raw chicken.

2. Preheat the oven to 400°F. Line a standard 18 by 13-inch baking sheet with parchment paper.

3. Arrange the chicken on the prepared pan, draining off and discarding its marinade.

4. Transfer the pan to the oven and bake the chicken until an instant-read thermometer reaches 165°F, 17 to 20 minutes. To achieve darker browning, switch the oven to broil and place the pan beneath the heat source for 1 to 3 minutes, watching carefully. Remove the pan from the oven.

5. Serve the chicken with the reserved marinade as a drizzling sauce or dip.

Change It Up

Air-fry it: Arrange the chicken pieces in a single layer in an air fryer and cook at 375°F for about 12 minutes. You may need to cook in two or three batches, depending on the size of your air fryer.

Vinaigrette Chicken: Substitute red wine or white wine vinegar for the lemon juice.

CREAMY LEMON SHRIMP & ZUCCHINI

Frozen wild shrimp are one of my go-to proteins when I need dinner to be ready in under 30 minutes. And this is one of my favorite ways to cook them, as a quick skillet meal that's heavy on the veggies and low on the carbs. It yields a gorgeous, creamy sauce that you won't want to let go to waste. To soak it up, I usually serve it with roasted spaghetti squash or cauliflower rice, keeping the dish low carb, but sometimes I opt for rice, orzo, or another cooked grain instead.

Serves 4
Ready in 30 minutes

1½ pounds peeled and deveined wild shrimp
1 teaspoon fine sea salt
1 teaspoon paprika
3 tablespoons Greek olive oil
3 medium zucchini (about 1½ pounds), cubed
1 medium red bell pepper, diced
½ cup white wine or vegetable broth
3 garlic cloves, minced
Freshly ground black pepper
½ cup heavy cream
Grated zest and juice of 1 medium lemon
1 teaspoon Dijon mustard
½ cup grated Parmesan cheese
Fresh basil leaves, for garnish
Lemon wedges, for squeezing

1. Pat the shrimp dry with paper towels. In a bowl, toss the shrimp with ½ teaspoon of the salt and the paprika.

2. Preheat a wide skillet over medium-high heat until hot. Swirl in 2 tablespoons of the oil. Add the shrimp, spreading them out evenly in the pan, and cook undisturbed for 90 seconds, until pink. Flip them over and repeat, until they're fully cooked and pink all over. Transfer them to a plate and cover to keep warm.

3. Add the remaining 1 tablespoon oil to the pan. Add the zucchini, bell pepper, and wine and sauté until the veggies are crisp-tender, about 5 minutes. Stir in the garlic and pepper to taste. Add the cream, lemon zest and juice, mustard, and Parmesan. Return the shrimp to the pan and season with the remaining ½ teaspoon salt. Simmer for another 3 to 4 minutes to meld the flavors. and adjust the seasoning as needed.

4. Garnish with the basil and serve immediately along with lemon wedges for squeezing.

BOYFRIEND STEAK SKILLET
with Peppers & Feta

When I was in college in New York City, I had a very tiny kitchenette in my apartment. There was a hot plate, a small sink, a mini fridge—and nothing else. While living there, I decided to cook for my boyfriend, whom I seriously wanted to impress. But at that point in my life, I hardly knew how to cook. Thankfully, he knew his way around the kitchen (even my tiny one), and that night he taught me how to make this flavorful stir-fry of steak and veggies, insisting at the end on the addition of feta, which softened and melted to perfection. My mind was blown by the delicious flavors, and to this day I still make it, sometimes substituting shrimp or chicken for the steak.

Serves 4
Ready in 30 minutes, not including marinating time

Marinated Steak
2 tablespoons balsamic vinegar
2 tablespoons Greek olive oil
1 tablespoon Worcestershire sauce
1 tablespoon tamari or reduced-sodium soy sauce
1 teaspoon Dijon mustard
2 garlic cloves, minced
1½ pounds sirloin steak, fat trimmed, sliced into thin strips

Stir-Fry
2 tablespoons Greek olive oil
1 large sweet onion, sliced
1 large red or orange bell pepper, thinly sliced
8 ounces cremini mushrooms, sliced
Fine sea salt and freshly ground black pepper
3 garlic cloves, minced
2 tablespoons unsalted butter
5 ounces Greek feta cheese, cut into small cubes
Balsamic glaze, for drizzling
Toasted sesame seeds, for sprinkling

1. To marinate the steak: In a bowl, whisk together the balsamic vinegar, oil, Worcestershire sauce, tamari, mustard, and garlic. Add the steak strips, tossing to combine. Marinate for at least 1 hour or up to 8 hours in the refrigerator.

2. To make the stir-fry: Preheat a wide skillet over medium-high heat until hot. Swirl in the oil. Add the onion, bell pepper, and mushrooms and sauté, stirring often, until the vegetables are crisp-tender, 7 to 9 minutes. Season with salt and pepper to taste. Stir in the garlic and once it's fragrant, scrape all the vegetables onto a plate.

3. Return the pan to the heat and add 1 tablespoon of the butter. Use a slotted spoon to lift about half of the steak strips from the marinade and add them to the pan. Sear until nicely browned on both sides, 1 to 2 minutes per side. Move the cooked steak to the plate with the vegetables and repeat this process, using the remaining 1 tablespoon butter and steak strips (discard the remaining marinade). Stir all the steak and vegetables together in the pan and turn off the heat. Sprinkle the feta over the top and cover the pan for a minute or two to allow the cheese to soften slightly.

4. Divide the steak and vegetables among four dinner plates. Serve hot, drizzled with the balsamic glaze and a sprinkling of sesame seeds.

Change It Up

Easy swaps: Substitute whole shrimp or bite-size pieces of chicken thighs or breasts for the steak.

ZUCCHINI & PROSCIUTTO "LASAGNA" LOAF

FAN FAVORITE

Most people don't think it's possible to make a super-flavorful, vegetable-centric pan of lasagna in 30 minutes flat. But this viral recipe shows that it can, in fact, be done! It has a couple tricks up its sleeve, such as using quick-cooking, lightly breaded zucchini strips as the lasagna noodles, as well as rich, salty-sweet prosciutto for fast flavor. And a loaf pan, being the ideal size for four or five servings, helps things to cook quickly. That said, it's an easy recipe to customize, layering in extra vegetables to make it a vegetarian lasagna or using sliced deli ham or turkey instead of prosciutto.

Serves 5
Ready in 30 minutes

Olive oil cooking spray, for spraying the parchment
3 medium zucchini (6 to 8 ounces each)
½ cup fine dried bread crumbs
⅓ cup grated Parmesan cheese
¾ teaspoon dried parsley
½ teaspoon garlic powder
½ teaspoon onion powder
½ teaspoon paprika
Fine sea salt
6 thin slices prosciutto
2 cups shredded mozzarella cheese (8 ounces)
1 tablespoon Greek olive oil
Red chile flakes, for sprinkling

Change It Up

Make it gluten-free: Substitute superfine almond flour for the bread crumbs.

Make it vegetarian: Omit the prosciutto, laying in your favorite well-seasoned, flavorful veggies, like sautéed mushrooms, caramelized onions, or roasted winter squash (they'll need to compensate for the super-flavorful prosciutto).

1. Preheat the oven to 350°F. Line a 9 by 5-inch loaf pan with parchment paper on all sides (see my parchment-lining tip on page 40) and spray it lightly with the cooking spray.

2. Use a vegetable peeler or mandoline to slice the zucchini lengthwise into long thin pieces, ideally between 1/16 and 1/8 inch thick. Discard the outer skin slices. Pat the slices dry using paper towels.

3. On a plate, combine the bread crumbs, Parmesan, parsley, garlic powder, onion powder, paprika, and a few pinches of salt. Dredge the zucchini in the bread crumb mixture, pressing each piece to adhere as well as possible.

4. Sprinkle 1 to 2 tablespoons of the remaining bread crumb mixture on the bottom of the prepared pan. Layer in one-third of the zucchini pieces, overlapping them as needed. Arrange three slices of prosciutto on top, scrunching them up to create a bit of volume, and then sprinkle with one-third of the mozzarella. Repeat once more with another layer of zucchini, the remaining prosciutto, and more mozzarella. Top with the remaining zucchini, mozzarella, and any remaining bread crumb mixture. Drizzle with the oil and sprinkle with a few pinches of chile flakes.

5. Transfer the pan to the oven and bake until the cheese is bubbling at the edges and the lasagna is browned all over, 24 to 26 minutes.

6. Remove the pan from the oven and let the lasagna cool in the pan for 10 to 15 minutes to set.

7. Using the parchment paper, lift the lasagna onto a serving platter or cutting board. Slice and serve hot or warm.

HONEY-ROASTED SALMON-FARRO BOWLS
with Radishes & Broccolini

An air fryer helps to make this bowl-style dinner super fast and absolutely bursting with unique flavors. If you've never tried roasting radishes, know that heat makes them much milder and more succulent, and the honey in the marinade beautifully bridges their flavor with the salmon and broccolini. Use broccoli florets cut into small (½- to ¾-inch) pieces in place of broccolini if you can't find it and remember that you can always ask your fishmonger to trim off the salmon skin for you to help save a little prep time.

Serves 4
Ready in 20 to 45 minutes

Fine sea salt
1½ cups farro
3 tablespoons honey
2 tablespoons Greek olive oil
1 teaspoon paprika
1 teaspoon dried oregano
Freshly ground black pepper
1½ pounds wild salmon, skin removed and cut into 1½-inch cubes
2 small bunches of broccolini (about 12 ounces total), cut into ½-inch pieces
1 bunch of radishes, quartered

Toppings
1 medium cucumber, peeled, seeded, and sliced into thin half-moons
1 avocado, cubed
Favorite Pickled Red Onions (page 119), for serving
Lazy Tzatziki (page 200), for serving
Toasted white or black sesame seeds, for garnish
Lime wedges, for squeezing

1. To cook the farro: Bring a medium saucepan full of water to a boil, then salt it generously and add the farro. After the water comes back to a boil, turn down the heat to maintain a gentle simmer, partially cover the pan, and cook until the grains are tender, using the package instructions as a guide (the timing will range from 12 minutes for pearled grains to 40 minutes for whole farro). Drain thoroughly, then return the cooked farro to the covered pan to keep it warm.

2. Meanwhile, preheat an air fryer to 375°F (see Change It Up below for using a traditional oven).

3. In a bowl, whisk together the honey, oil, paprika, oregano, ¾ teaspoon salt, and several grinds of pepper. Add the salmon, broccolini, and radishes and stir until everything is evenly coated. Spread into an even layer in the air fryer basket (cooking in two batches if necessary, depending on its size, to avoid crowding) and air-fry until the salmon is just cooked through, 8 to 12 minutes, stirring once halfway.

4. Divide the cooked farro among bowls and top with the salmon and vegetables along with the cucumber, avocado, a scoop of pickled onions, spoonfuls of tzatziki, and a sprinkling of sesame seeds. Serve with lime wedges for squeezing.

Change It Up

To use a traditional oven: Preheat the oven to 375°F with convection, or to 400°F without convection. Line a standard 18 by 13-inch baking sheet with parchment paper. Spread out the salmon and vegetables on the prepared pan and bake until the salmon is cooked through, adding an extra 2 to 5 minutes to the air-frying time as needed.

Easy swaps: Substitute cod, haddock, or sea bass for the salmon. Swap the farro with your favorite grain, such as barley, brown rice, or quinoa.

CRUNCHY BAKED BEEF SOUVLAKI TACOS

Inspired by the flavors of souvlaki, these crunchy tacos, which are filled with juicy spiced meat, melty and crispy cheese, are just impossible to stop eating. And after you've cooked the ground meat, they come together very simply on just a sheet pan. As far as condiments go, although salsa would be a good option in addition to the tzatziki, I'm partial to this easy tomato relish instead. If using tortillas smaller than 6 inches, you can make 10 to 12 tacos; thin tortillas will achieve the best crispiness.

Makes 8 tacos
Ready in 50 minutes

Meat Filling
1 tablespoon Greek olive oil
1 pound ground beef (95/5)
1 tablespoon tomato paste
1 teaspoon onion powder
¾ teaspoon fine sea salt
¾ teaspoon ground cumin
½ teaspoon garlic powder
½ teaspoon paprika
½ teaspoon ground cinnamon
⅛ teaspoon ground cloves

Tomato Relish
2 medium tomatoes, seeded and finely diced
2 tablespoons finely diced red onion
2 tablespoons chopped fresh parsley
2 teaspoons red wine vinegar
Fine sea salt

Assembly
8 (6-inch) thin corn or flour tortillas
Olive oil cooking spray, for spraying the tortillas
2 cups shredded Mexican cheese blend or Cheddar cheese (8 ounces)
¼ cup pitted and chopped Kalamata olives
2 scallions, green and white parts, thinly sliced

Lazy Tzatziki (page 200), for garnish

1. Preheat the oven to 425°F. Line a standard 18 by 13-inch sheet pan with parchment paper.

2. To make the meat filling: Preheat a medium skillet over medium heat until hot. Swirl in the oil and add the beef, tomato paste, onion powder, salt, and all the spices. Brown the meat, stirring often to combine and break it up into crumbles, until it's fully cooked through, 7 to 10 minutes. Carefully drain off or blot away any grease that's collected in the pan.

3. Meanwhile, to make the tomato relish: In a small bowl, combine the tomatoes, onion, parsley, vinegar, and salt to taste. Taste and adjust the seasoning as needed.

4. To assemble: Arrange the tortillas on the prepared sheet pan (a little overlap is fine) and spray them lightly with the cooking spray. Flip them over and sprinkle each one evenly with the cheese, olives, and scallions.

5. Transfer the pan to the oven and bake the tortillas just until the cheese is melted, 3 to 5 minutes.

6. Remove the pan from the oven. Divide the beef over the tortillas, arranging some on one half of each tortilla, then use a spatula to fold the exposed half over the meat, pressing down on it gently to make a compact taco.

7. Return the pan to the oven and bake until the tortillas are golden and crunchy, 18 to 22 minutes more. Remove the pan from the oven.

8. Serve the tacos hot or warm, garnished with the tomato relish and tzatziki.

Change It Up

Easy swaps: Use any ground meat you like such as lamb, chicken, or pork. Just be sure to thoroughly drain higher-fat meat before assembling the tacos.

COASTAL BAKED COD

One of my family's go-to dinners, this baked cod could not be simpler to make. There's hardly any chopping or prep; everything just gets added to the pan and baked in the oven—and what emerges is beautiful and delicious enough to serve at dinner parties. Add salt carefully, since there is plenty of briny flavor from the capers and the olives. And while we love cod fillets because they're so easy to find and pair nicely with these Mediterranean flavors, any white fish, or even salmon, works just as well.

Serves 4
Ready in 25 minutes

1 pint cherry tomatoes, halved
1 small red onion, thinly sliced into strips
3 garlic cloves, minced
8 green Greek olives
8 Kalamata olives
1 tablespoon capers, drained
3 tablespoons Greek olive oil
1 tablespoon red wine vinegar
1 lemon, sliced into thin rounds
4 cod fillets (about 8 ounces each)
Fine sea salt and freshly ground black pepper
5 sprigs of thyme
Fresh thyme leaves, for garnish

1. Preheat the oven to 425°F.

2. In a medium bowl, combine the tomatoes, onion, garlic, Greek and Kalamata olives, capers, oil, and vinegar.

3. Scatter the lemon slices in the bottom of a 9 by 13-inch baking dish, then arrange the fish fillets on top. Season the fish lightly with salt and pepper. Spoon the tomato-olive mixture all around the fish evenly, including any juices at the bottom of the bowl. Scatter the thyme sprigs on top.

4. Transfer the dish to the oven and bake until the fillets are just set and easily flake in their centers, 12 to 15 minutes. Remove the pan from the oven.

5. Serve hot or warm, garnished with the thyme leaves and more pepper.

SEARED SCALLOPS
over Creamy Zucchini Couscous

Here's an elegant, restaurant-quality meal that, just from tasting it, you'd never imagine to be so simple. It's also a great example of how versatile and unique zucchini is, because it's what helps create an incredibly creamy, savory sauce that needs no actual cream. I love pearl couscous here for its substantial chew, but if you can't find it, substitute orzo. Note that for an attractive golden-brown sear on the scallops, it's very important to make sure they are *dry*. Be thorough as you blot them with paper towels.

Serves 4
Ready in 40 minutes

- 2½ cups low-sodium chicken broth or water (or a combination)
- ⅓ cup plus 2 tablespoons Greek olive oil
- 1½ cups pearl couscous
- Fine sea salt
- 3 medium zucchini (6 to 8 ounces each), thinly sliced into rounds
- ½ teaspoon red chile flakes
- 3 garlic cloves, minced
- Freshly ground black pepper
- 1½ pounds sea scallops
- ½ cup freshly grated Parmesan cheese
- Grated lemon zest, for garnish
- Crispy Shallots (page 212), for garnish
- Lemon wedges, for squeezing

1. In a medium saucepan, bring the chicken broth to a boil. Add 1 tablespoon of the oil, the couscous, and ½ teaspoon salt. Turn down the heat to a simmer, cover, and simmer gently until the couscous is tender, about 10 minutes (or according to package directions). Transfer to a serving bowl.

2. Preheat a wide nonstick skillet over medium heat until it's hot. Add ⅓ cup of the olive oil, the zucchini, and chile flakes. Sauté, stirring periodically, until the zucchini is soft and tender, about 10 minutes. Stir in the garlic and season with salt and pepper to taste.

3. Set aside about ¼ cup of the zucchini, then scrape all the remaining contents of the pan into a blender and puree until creamy and smooth. Pour this sauce onto the cooked couscous, add the reserved zucchini, and toss to combine.

4. Blot the scallops *thoroughly* dry with paper towels—if they're not dry, you won't get a golden-brown sear. Season them all over with pinches of salt and pepper.

5. Wipe the nonstick skillet clean and set over medium heat. Once hot, swirl in the remaining 1 tablespoon oil. Arrange the scallops in the pan in an even layer, spacing them out to avoid crowding. Sear without disturbing until they're golden brown on the bottoms, about 3 minutes. Gently flip them and repeat to sear the opposite sides.

6. To serve, divide the couscous among four dinner plates and top with the Parmesan. Arrange the scallops on top of the couscous and garnish with the lemon zest and crispy shallots. Serve with lemon wedges on the side for squeezing.

MEDITERRANEAN MEATLOAF

Growing up in a Greek community on Long Island, I did not eat meatloaf as a kid because that was always thought to be very much an American dish. But as an adult, it's one that I have really adopted as my own, and I love it as an easy, high-protein main dish for weeknights. I also think it's a perfect vessel for Greek flavors like Kalamata olives, feta, and oregano, with tzatziki served on the side. As a nod to the classic, I give you the option of an American-style, ketchup-based glaze, which I am partial to, but it's easy to leave out, based on your preferences.

Serves 6
Ready in 1 hour 15 minutes

2 tablespoons Greek olive oil
1 medium sweet onion, diced
3 garlic cloves, minced
1 teaspoon dried oregano
1 pound ground lamb
1 pound ground beef (95/5)
¾ cup fine dried bread crumbs
2 large eggs, lightly beaten
1 tablespoon balsamic vinegar
⅓ cup Kalamata or green olives, pitted and diced
4 ounces Greek feta cheese, crumbled (about 1 cup)
3 tablespoons chopped fresh parsley, plus more for garnish
1½ teaspoons fine sea salt
Freshly ground black pepper

Glaze (optional)
¼ cup ketchup
2 tablespoons honey
2 tablespoons balsamic vinegar
2 teaspoons Worcestershire sauce

Lazy Tzatziki (page 200), for serving

1. Preheat the oven to 350°F. Line a standard 18 by 13-inch sheet pan with parchment paper.

2. Preheat a medium skillet over medium heat until hot. Swirl in the oil. Add the onion and cook until just softened but not browned, about 4 minutes. Add the garlic and oregano and stir until fragrant, then scrape the mixture into a large bowl and set aside to cool slightly.

3. Add the ground meats, the bread crumbs, eggs, vinegar, olives, feta, and parsley to the bowl. Season with the salt and some pepper to taste. Gently combine without overmixing (I like to use my hands for this step). Shape the meat into an oblong football 8 to 10 inches long and flatten it out slightly, then place it in the center of the prepared pan.

4. To make the glaze (if using): In a small bowl, whisk together the ketchup, honey, vinegar, and Worcestershire sauce. Taste and adjust the seasoning as needed. Pour or brush the glaze on top of the meatloaf.

5. Transfer the pan to the oven and bake the meatloaf until fully cooked in the center and an instant-read thermometer reaches 160°F, about 1 hour. To achieve some browning on the glaze, switch the oven to broil and place the meatloaf beneath the heat source for 1 to 3 minutes, watching carefully.

6. Remove the pan from the oven and allow to rest for 10 minutes before slicing.

7. Serve hot with the tzatziki on the side.

Change It Up

Easy swaps: Any combination of ground turkey, chicken, pork, beef, or lamb all work great here.

Make it gluten-free: Substitute superfine almond flour for the bread crumbs.

THE BROILER TRICK If you've ever been frustrated that the food you cook doesn't look as golden brown and crispy as the recipe photo, the broiler is going to be your best friend. Simply switch your oven to broil and place the pan directly beneath the heat source. But don't go anywhere! Things will take on color and crispiness very quickly. It usually won't take longer than a minute or two.

WARM WINTER VEGETABLE SALAD
with Quinoa

Back in 2013, when I first created Hungry Happens, I had a major love affair with quinoa. I was following a more restrictive "clean eating" diet, where it figured prominently. My eating has since become much less rigid, but I continue to love quinoa for its unique flavor and quick cooking time. This salad combines a rich, easy tahini dressing and a medley of roasted veggies, allowing plenty of freedom to choose your favorites. It's best served warm, because that keeps things loose and creamy rather than dense and stiff. If you opt to skip the crunchy panko topping, replace it with another crunchy element, such as toasted nuts or seeds, or even my Tahini-Crusted Chickpeas (page 68).

Serves 4 to 6
Ready in 45 minutes

2 pounds sweet potatoes, winter squash, broccoli, and/or cauliflower, cut into ¾-inch cubes or small florets
3 tablespoons Greek olive oil
1 teaspoon dried oregano
1 teaspoon onion powder
½ teaspoon garlic powder
Fine sea salt and freshly ground black pepper
½ cup quinoa, rinsed and drained
¾ cup water

Dressing
3 tablespoons well-stirred tahini
3 tablespoons Greek olive oil
3 tablespoons fresh lemon juice (1½ medium lemons)
1 tablespoon maple syrup or honey
½ teaspoon fine sea salt

About ¼ cup Favorite Pickled Red Onions (page 119), drained
2 handfuls baby spinach or other tender salad greens (2 ounces), coarsely chopped
¼ cup chopped fresh parsley or dill
Crunchy Panko Topping (recipe follows), for garnish
Freshly ground black pepper, for garnish

1. Preheat the oven to 400°F. Line a standard 18 by 13-inch baking sheet with parchment paper.

2. In a large bowl, toss together the cubed vegetables, the oil, oregano, onion powder, garlic powder, ¾ teaspoon salt, and pepper to taste. Spread out the vegetables in an even layer on the prepared baking sheet.

3. Transfer the pan to the oven and roast until everything is tender and lightly browned, 25 to 35 minutes, stirring the vegetables once.

4. Meanwhile, in a small saucepan, combine the quinoa, water, and a few pinches of salt. Bring to a boil, then immediately turn down the heat to low, cover, and simmer gently until the quinoa is tender and the liquid is absorbed, 15 to 18 minutes.

5. To make the dressing: While the quinoa cooks, in a small bowl, whisk together all the ingredients until smooth. Add water by the teaspoon to make a runnier consistency, if desired.

6. Remove the pan from the oven and spoon the roasted vegetables into a large salad bowl. Add the quinoa, pickled onions, spinach, and parsley. Toss with dressing to taste.

7. Serve warm, garnished with the crunchy panko and pepper.

CRUNCHY PANKO TOPPING
Makes 1 cup

1 cup panko bread crumbs
2 tablespoons Greek olive oil
Fine sea salt
Grated zest of ½ lemon

1. In a medium skillet, combine the panko, oil, and a few pinches of salt and stir to coat the panko evenly. Toast over medium-low heat, stirring constantly, until the panko is golden brown.

2. Remove the pan from the heat, stir in the lemon zest, and scrape the mixture onto a plate to cool completely. Store in an airtight container at room temperature for up to 3 days.

BROCCOLI-FETA SOUP

In my house, feta goes with pretty much everything. But if putting feta in soup is new for you, you're in for a treat. On top of being easy, this popular recipe is so creamy and comforting, thanks to the rich and tangy flavor of the cheese. It has plenty of great texture, too, so that it's hearty, filling, and features a pretty good dose of greens. It's important to stir often if not *constantly* as you add the orzo, because otherwise the pasta can clump and stick to the pot. And when you serve it, make sure there's fresh crusty bread on the side for dunking!

Serves 4
Ready in 1 hour

- 1 pound broccoli, florets and stalks chopped into small pieces
- 3 garlic cloves, minced
- 4 cups low-sodium chicken broth
- 2 cups water
- 1 teaspoon fine sea salt
- Freshly ground black pepper
- ¾ cup orzo
- 4 ounces Greek feta cheese, crumbled (about 1 cup)
- Greek olive oil, for drizzling
- Lemon wedges, for squeezing
- Red chile flakes, for garnish

1. In a soup pot, combine the broccoli, garlic, broth, water, salt, and pepper to taste. Bring to a boil. Turn down the heat to a simmer, cover, and simmer until the broccoli is very tender, about 30 minutes, stirring occasionally.

2. Using a potato masher or the back of a wooden spoon, gently mash the broccoli to thicken the soup slightly. But don't mash it too much—you want large and small pieces for texture.

3. With the soup simmering, stir in the orzo and cook, uncovered, stirring often until the pasta is cooked, about 15 minutes. Remove the pot from the heat and stir in the feta.

4. Serve hot, drizzled with the oil, spritzes of lemon juice, and pinches of chile flakes for garnish.

Note: If you buy broccoli stalks (which, unlike crowns, have their thick stems attached), don't throw the stems away! Just peel off the outer skin with a vegetable peeler, chop them up into small pieces, and add them to the pot along with the florets.

Change It Up

Amp it up: Add 1 to 2 cups shredded rotisserie chicken or 2 cans drained and rinsed chickpeas to boost the protein.

Make it gluten-free: Swap white rice for the orzo.

GO GREEK

Food is so central to my Greek upbringing that no cookbook of mine would be complete without a chapter devoted to Greek recipes. Collected here are my most favorite comfort dishes, like Avgolemono (page 123), Soutzoukakia (page 111), and Ladenia (page 133), which remind me poignantly of home because my yiayia and my mom used to make them for me, and now I make them for my kids. Others, like my Loaf Pan Chicken Gyros (page 103), Lazy Spanakopita (page 124), and Easier Skillet Moussaka (page 107), are what I call "Stella spins," where I've reformatted classic dishes for the modern-day, more time-crunched home kitchen. In both cases, you simply can't go wrong when it comes to bold, fresh Greek flavors.

LOAF PAN CHICKEN GYROS

You absolutely must get gyros if you visit Greece. They're the most popular street food, always inexpensive and delicious. They're made by slowly roasting meat that's been threaded onto a large vertical skewer, then sliced off in shavings, piled onto a pita, and loaded up with as many condiments as will fit (French fries are a must for me). They aren't so easy to make at home in the traditional way, but this loaf pan workaround is one of my very popular recipes that give gyros a home-cook friendly, healthier spin without sacrificing any of the juicy, tender deliciousness. It's worth flagging this recipe just for the marinade—it works great for simple grilled or baked chicken, too.

Serves 4
Ready in 1 hour 20 minutes, not including marinating time

Marinated Chicken
3 tablespoons whole milk Greek yogurt
4 garlic cloves, minced
1 tablespoon Greek olive oil
1 tablespoon white wine vinegar
2 tablespoons fresh lemon juice (1 medium lemon)
1 tablespoon dried oregano
1 teaspoon paprika
2 teaspoons fine sea salt
½ teaspoon freshly ground black pepper
2 pounds boneless, skinless chicken thighs, patted dry

Suggested Accompaniments
1 large beefsteak tomato, sliced
1 small red onion, thinly sliced
Chopped fresh parsley
Warmed pitas
Crispy Baked French Fries (page 165)
Lazy Tzatziki (page 200)

1. To marinate the chicken: In a small bowl or measuring glass, whisk together the yogurt, garlic, oil, vinegar, lemon juice, oregano, paprika, salt, and pepper. Place the chicken in a large resealable bag, then add the marinade. Seal the bag, pressing out as much air as possible, and, using your hands, gently massage the chicken so it's evenly coated. Transfer to the refrigerator for at least 2 hours or up to overnight.

2. Preheat the oven to 350°F. Line a 9 by 5-inch loaf pan with parchment paper (see my parchment-lining tip on page 40).

3. Layer the chicken into the loaf pan and discard the remaining marinade. Use your hands or a spatula to gently pack the meat down so it's compressed into an even layer.

4. Transfer the pan to the oven and bake until the meat is fully cooked in the center and an instant-read thermometer reaches 160°F, about 1 hour.

5. Remove the pan from the oven and let rest in the pan for 10 minutes. Carefully pour off and discard any juices that collect in the pan. Unmold the chicken, using the overhanging parchment to lift it out, then set it on a cutting board.

6. Slice the meat thinly and serve warm, with any or all of the suggested accompaniments.

Change It Up

Easy swaps: Substitute 2 pounds boneless, skinless chicken breasts, butterflied or sliced into thin cutlets, or thin-cut boneless loin pork chops (also called center-cut) for the chicken thighs.

CHICKEN FASOLAKIA
Green Bean Stew

Fasolakia is a very popular Greek dish, essentially summer in a skillet. It's traditionally made when green beans are abundant and always with plenty of vibrant, fresh Greek olive oil. My family adds chicken pieces to the dish, braising them with the beans so that all the flavors meld (this is the kind of dish that gets better as it sits). This has the extra advantage of turning what might have been a side dish into a hearty, nearly complete dinner unto itself. Just serve it with feta cheese and fresh, crusty bread for mopping up the sauce.

Serves 4
Ready in 50 minutes

1 tablespoon potato starch or all-purpose flour
2 pounds boneless, skinless chicken thighs, cut in half and patted dry
5 tablespoons Greek olive oil
1 medium sweet onion, diced
1 large carrot, cut into bite-size chunks
3 garlic cloves, minced
1 tablespoon tomato paste
1 (14.5-ounce) can diced tomatoes, preferably fire-roasted
1½ cups low-sodium chicken broth or water
1 tablespoon granulated sugar
Fine sea salt and freshly ground black pepper
1 pound green beans, stemmed
¼ cup chopped fresh parsley

1. Sprinkle the potato starch all over the chicken thighs, using your hands to ensure that they're coated evenly.

2. Preheat a large deep braiser or Dutch oven over medium-high heat until hot. Swirl in 1 tablespoon of the oil. Add the chicken, arranging it in an even layer, and sear until golden all over, 3 to 4 minutes per side (it doesn't need to be fully cooked at this point). Transfer the chicken to a plate.

3. Return the pot to the heat and swirl in the remaining 4 tablespoons oil. Add the onion and carrot and sauté until they're beginning to soften, 3 to 5 minutes. Stir in the garlic, followed by the tomato paste.

4. Return the chicken to the pot along with the tomatoes, broth, sugar, and pinches of salt and pepper to taste. Bring to a boil. Turn down the heat to a simmer and cook for 5 minutes. Add the green beans, cover the pot, and cook, gently stirring occasionally, until the green beans are fork-tender and the flavors have melded, about 30 minutes.

5. Just before serving, stir in the parsley. Divide the chicken and beans among bowls and serve with the sauce from the pot spooned over the top.

Change It Up

Beef Fasolakia: Substitute 2 pounds cubed beef stew meat or shoulder cuts for the chicken.

EASIER SKILLET MOUSSAKA

Like lasagna, moussaka is known to be a project dish, requiring several different components and a whole setup for the assembly. There's the fragrant, seasoned meat, the tender eggplant and potatoes, the tomato sauce, and a blanket of béchamel; it can all be a lot. This skillet moussaka streamlines things by putting most of the action into just one pan, making it more suitable for weeknights or for when you get a sudden craving, but it's just as much of a comfort as the more laborious, time-consuming kind.

Serves 6
Ready in 2 hours

1 medium eggplant (about 1 pound), cut into 1½-inch chunks
Fine sea salt
¼ cup Greek olive oil
1 pound baby potatoes, halved, or Yukon golds, cubed
½ teaspoon paprika
Freshly ground black pepper
1 medium sweet onion, diced
4 garlic cloves, minced
2 tablespoons tomato paste
1 pound ground lamb or ground beef (95/5)
½ teaspoon ground cinnamon
¼ teaspoon ground allspice
Pinch of ground cloves
1 (28-ounce) can crushed tomatoes
1 teaspoon honey or granulated sugar, plus more as needed (optional)
2 tablespoons chopped fresh parsley

Béchamel

4 tablespoons unsalted butter
6 tablespoons all-purpose flour
4½ cups whole milk
Pinch of ground nutmeg
Fine sea salt
¼ cup grated Parmesan cheese
Chopped fresh parsley, for garnish

1. Place the eggplant pieces on a large kitchen towel and sprinkle lightly all over with salt. Let them sit for 15 to 20 minutes and then blot away all the surface moisture.

2. Preheat a wide deep ovenproof pan, such as a braiser, over medium-high heat until hot. Swirl in 1 tablespoon of the oil, then add the potatoes, paprika, ½ teaspoon salt, and a few grinds of pepper to taste. Cook, stirring often, until the potatoes are lightly browned, 8 to 10 minutes. Transfer the potatoes to a plate.

3. Swirl 2 tablespoons of the oil into the pan and add the eggplant. Sauté, stirring often, until browned and just fork-tender, 8 to 10 minutes. Transfer the eggplant to the plate with the potatoes.

4. Swirl the remaining 1 tablespoon oil into the pan, add the onion and sauté until soft and translucent, 4 to 5 minutes. Stir in the garlic and tomato paste. Add the ground meat and cook it until it's no longer pink, breaking it into crumbles, 5 to 6 minutes.

5. Stir in the cinnamon, allspice, cloves, ¾ teaspoon salt, and pepper to taste. Pour in the tomatoes and bring to a boil. Turn down the heat to a simmer and cook uncovered until the sauce thickens, 12 to 15 minutes. Stir in the honey, if using, and the parsley. Taste and adjust the seasoning as needed. Remove the pan from the heat.

6. Push the meat sauce to one side of the pan and add the potatoes and eggplant. Nudge the ground meat mixture over the top of the vegetables, so they're mostly covered.

7. Preheat the oven to 400°F.

8. To make the béchamel: In a medium saucepan over medium heat, melt the butter. Sprinkle in the flour and stir until a smooth paste forms, about 1 minute. Gradually stir in the milk and increase the heat slightly to bring the mixture just to a boil, then turn down the heat and stir constantly until it thickens enough to coat the back of a spoon. Season with the nutmeg and salt to taste.

9. Ladle the béchamel evenly over the meat and sprinkle with the Parmesan. Transfer the pan to the oven and bake the moussaka until golden brown on top, 25 to 30 minutes.

10. Remove from the oven and rest for 30 minutes. Slice and serve warm, garnished with the parsley.

YIANNIS'S FAVORITE PORK SOUVLAKI WRAPS

My son, Yiannis, loves a souvlaki wrap, that late-night street-food staple of grilled meat, wrapped up in a warm flatbread with different toppings and, ideally, a big handful of french fries. I've created this recipe for him, and it's actually much easier than you might think if you remember to get the pork marinating in advance. I prefer lavash as the wrap—it's thinner and more pliable than a pita, and it allows you to roll up the wrap like a burrito. And if you want to go the french fry route, use my Crispy Baked French Fries on page 165.

Serves 4
Ready in 30 minutes, not including marinating time

Pork Souvlaki
- 2 pounds pork tenderloin or boneless pork loin roast, patted dry
- ½ cup Greek olive oil
- 2 tablespoons fresh lemon juice (1 medium lemon)
- 2 tablespoons red wine vinegar
- 4 garlic cloves, smashed
- 2 teaspoons fine sea salt
- 2 teaspoons dried oregano
- 1 teaspoon freshly ground black pepper

Assembly
- 4 lavash flatbreads
- Easy Lemony Hummus (recipe follows)
- Thinly sliced romaine lettuce
- Diced tomato or halved cherry tomatoes
- Favorite Pickled Red Onions (page 119) or thinly sliced red onion
- Lazy Tzatziki (page 200), for topping
- Balsamic glaze, for drizzling
- Greek olive oil, for drizzling
- Chopped fresh parsley, for garnish

1. Slice the pork tenderloin crosswise into ¾-inch-thick rounds, then cut each round into strips about ¾ inch thick.

2. In a measuring glass, whisk together the oil, lemon juice, vinegar, garlic, salt, oregano, and pepper. Put the cubed pork in a resealable plastic bag, then pour the marinade over it. Seal the bag and gently massage the meat to make sure it's evenly coated. Allow the pork to marinate for at least 1 hour in the refrigerator or up to 1 day.

3. Preheat a wide skillet over medium heat. Place the lavash flatbreads, one at a time, into the dry pan to warm, flipping them a few times, until they are soft and heated through. Stack the warmed flatbreads on a plate and cover with a clean kitchen towel to keep them warm.

4. Increase the heat to medium-high and once the pan is hot, add as much of the pork (drained of its marinade) as will fit without crowding and cook until lightly browned and cooked through, 2 to 4 minutes per side. Move the cooked pork to a plate or platter and cover with aluminum foil to keep it warm. Repeat with the remaining pork.

5. To assemble the wraps: Smear some hummus over the middle of each lavash, followed by the lettuce, tomato, and pickled red onions. Top with a few pieces of pork, tzatziki, and a drizzle of balsamic glaze. Drizzle with the oil and sprinkle with the parsley, then roll up each lavash into a log and serve right away.

EASY LEMONY HUMMUS
Makes about 2 cups

- ¼ cup fresh lemon juice (2 medium lemons)
- 2 garlic cloves, coarsely chopped
- ½ teaspoon fine sea salt
- ½ cup well-stirred tahini
- 1 (15-ounce) can chickpeas, drained and rinsed
- 6 to 8 tablespoons hot tap water

In a blender or food processor, combine the lemon juice, garlic, salt, tahini, and chickpeas, in that order, and begin processing, scraping the sides as needed. With the motor running, add the water, about 2 tablespoons at a time, until a smooth and light consistency is achieved; this will take 2 to 3 minutes. Taste for seasoning and add more salt or lemon juice as needed.

Change It Up

Easy swaps: Use pork neck or shoulder cuts for richer meat; top-sirloin steak, cut into strips; or cubed chicken thighs or breasts.

SOUTZOUKAKIA
Baked Meatballs & Potatoes

FAN FAVORITE

I ate soutzoukakia all the time while growing up, and my yiayia always made the meatballs so perfectly tender and full of flavor. When made right, they really do melt in your mouth, and, as they cook in the oven, the potatoes soak up the meat's flavorful juices. With a simple green salad on the side, such as Yiayia's Maroulosalata (page 216), you've got a complete dinner that everyone will love. It's important to get the size right on the meatballs—they should be somewhere between a meatball and a burger patty, with the most important thing being that they're large enough so they don't dry out.

Serves 6
Ready in 1 hour 20 minutes

Marinated Potatoes
½ cup Greek olive oil
¼ cup fresh lemon juice (2 medium lemons)
¼ cup chopped fresh oregano, plus more for garnish
1½ teaspoons fine sea salt
3 pounds Yukon gold potatoes, peeled and cut into 1½-inch chunks

Meatballs
1 pound ground pork
1 pound ground beef (95/5)
2 large eggs
1 small sweet onion, finely chopped
1 bunch of fresh mint, finely minced
3 tablespoons Greek olive oil
1 large garlic clove, minced
1 cup fine dried bread crumbs
2 teaspoons red wine vinegar
2 teaspoons fine sea salt
½ teaspoon ground cumin
¼ teaspoon red chile flakes

1. Preheat the oven to 450°F.

2. To make the marinade: In a large bowl, whisk together the oil, lemon juice, oregano, and salt. Measure out 2 tablespoons of the marinade and set aside in a separate small bowl. Add the potatoes to the large bowl and toss to combine.

3. To make the meatballs: In another large bowl, use your hands to combine the ground meats, the eggs, onion, mint, oil, garlic, bread crumbs, vinegar, salt, cumin, and chile flakes. Divide into twelve portions and then shape them into oblong, sausage-shaped meatballs.

4. Arrange the meatballs in a 9 by 13-inch baking dish, spaced apart as well as possible, and drizzle with the reserved marinade. Scatter the potatoes between the meatballs, and pour in any marinade from the bowl. Tightly cover the dish with aluminum foil.

5. Transfer the dish to the oven and bake for 30 minutes. Turn down the oven temperature to 425°F and bake for 15 minutes more.

6. Uncover and bake until the meatballs are cooked through and golden brown, another 15 minutes or so. If you'd like to get a bit more browning, switch the oven to broil and place the pan beneath the heat source for 1 to 3 minutes, watching carefully. Remove the pan from the oven.

7. Serve hot, garnished with additional fresh oregano, spooning the sauce from the pan over each serving at the table.

Change It Up

Easy swaps: Any ground meat works here, such as lamb, chicken, turkey, or your favorite combination.

Make it gluten-free: Use superfine almond flour or gluten-free bread crumbs for the bread crumbs.

GREEK LAMB FRICASSEE

While it's a French dish, fricassee is very common in Greece, most often made with lamb. The meat becomes meltingly tender as it slowly cooks in a deeply flavorful sauce and like Avgolemono (page 123), it is thickened at the end with tempered eggs. If you've never tried it, you're in for a real treat. I make this for special occasions, but that doesn't mean it's fussy—it's a classic slow braise, with browned meat simply simmering away with a few easy-to-find ingredients that, with heat and time, meld into something very, very special. The only challenging part can be cutting up the leg of lamb, so I recommend asking your butcher to do that for you.

Serves 4 to 6
Ready in 1½ hours

3¼ pounds bone-in leg of lamb, cut into large pieces about 4 by 4 inches
1½ tablespoons Greek olive oil
Fine sea salt and freshly ground black pepper
4 cups low-sodium chicken broth
1 teaspoon garlic powder
2 bunches of scallions, green and white parts, thinly sliced
1 large head romaine lettuce, coarsely chopped
¼ cup plus 1 tablespoon chopped fresh dill, plus more for garnish
3 egg yolks, at room temperature
Grated zest of 1 large lemon
Juice of 2 large lemons
1 tablespoon tapioca starch or cornstarch
Lemon wedges, for squeezing

1. Coat the lamb pieces in the oil and season them well with salt and pepper.

2. Preheat a braiser or other large wide pot, such as a Dutch oven, over medium-high heat until hot. Add the lamb pieces in an even layer. Sear until browned all over, about 4 minutes per side.

3. Add the broth and garlic powder to the pot and bring to a boil. Turn down the heat to a gentle simmer, cover, and cook untouched until the meat is tender, about 1 hour 15 minutes.

4. Pile the scallions, romaine, and ¼ cup of the dill over the meat and cover it again, without stirring. Cook for 15 minutes more.

5. Meanwhile, in a small bowl, whisk together the egg yolks, lemon zest and juice, tapioca starch, the remaining 1 tablespoon dill, and a pinch or two of salt until smooth.

6. Slowly whisk about two ladlesful of hot broth from the pot into the lemon sauce to temper it. Remove the pot from the heat and pour in the lemon sauce all over. Carefully stir, gently swishing or swirling the pan back and forth to incorporate.

7. Serve right away, garnished with pepper and dill, with lemon wedges for squeezing on the side.

Change It Up

Swap the meat: Substitute cubed chuck roast, beef stew meat, bone-in chicken thighs, or drumsticks for the lamb, adjusting the cooking time in step 3 as necessary.

DECONSTRUCTED GEMISTA
Deconstructed Rice & Vegetable Stuffed Peppers

If you grew up Greek, you know all about gemista, the classic dish of herby rice-stuffed tomatoes, peppers, onions, and other vegetables. I was not a fan as a child, but as with many of these traditional dishes, I've come around in adulthood. My mom has always incorporated ground beef into the filling, and it is legendary, one of my most favorite meals. But when I want to replicate the experience of gemista in a hurry, I opt for an easier route. By deconstructing the dish, I've eliminated all the fussy assembly but held on to all the bold, fresh flavor, turning it into a one-pan, quick dinner that's high in protein and loaded with veggies.

Serves 4 to 6
Ready in 45 minutes

2 tablespoons Greek olive oil
1 pound ground beef (95/5)
1 medium sweet onion, diced
1 red bell pepper, diced
1 orange bell pepper, diced
½ teaspoon ground coriander
½ teaspoon ground cumin
½ teaspoon paprika
¼ teaspoon ground cinnamon
¼ teaspoon cayenne pepper
¼ teaspoon ground cloves
4 garlic cloves, minced
2 tablespoons tomato paste
¼ teaspoon red chile flakes
¾ teaspoon fine sea salt
Freshly ground black pepper
1 (14.5-ounce) can diced tomatoes, preferably fire-roasted
2 cups beef broth, plus more as needed, or water
1 small zucchini, shredded
1 cup basmati rice
2 tablespoons chopped fresh parsley, plus more for garnish
2 tablespoons chopped fresh mint
¼ cup grated Parmesan cheese
1 cup shredded mozzarella cheese

1. Preheat a large deep sauté pan or braiser over medium-high heat until hot. Swirl in 1 tablespoon of the oil, followed by the ground meat. Use a wooden spoon to break up the meat into crumbles and cook until it is no longer pink, 5 to 7 minutes. Transfer to a dish and cover to keep warm.

2. Add the remaining 1 tablespoon oil to the pan, followed by the onion, bell pepper, and spices. Sauté until the vegetables are just tender, 5 to 7 minutes. Stir in the garlic, tomato paste, chile flakes, salt, and a few grinds of pepper, stirring to combine. Add the tomatoes, broth, zucchini, and rice. Return the cooked beef to the pan. Bring the mixture to a boil. Turn down the heat to a gentle simmer, cover, and cook, without stirring, until the rice is tender, about 20 minutes. If the pan appears dry, sprinkle in 2 to 4 tablespoons more broth.

3. Stir in the parsley, mint, and Parmesan. Sprinkle the mozzarella over the surface and cover the pan to melt the cheese.

4. Remove the pan from the heat and garnish with more parsley.

5. Transfer to a serving bowl or platter if desired, and serve hot or warm.

Change It Up

Easy swaps: Use any ground meat you prefer, such as lamb, chicken, or turkey.

HALIBUT KLEFTIKO
Pesto Halibut Baked in Parchment

The Greek word *kleftiko* means "hidden," and in culinary uses, it refers to the traditional way of cooking a whole roast of lamb. Originally, the meat was cooked slowly in the ground with embers "hidden" under the dirt, but nowadays it's cooked in the oven but wrapped up (hidden!) in parchment. Using halibut instead of lamb as the protein makes this a much faster, lighter application of the technique, and it's a wonderful way to showcase good-quality fish because not a drop of flavor goes to waste, sealed up inside the packet in which it steams. While this recipe is easy enough for weeknights, it's definitely suitable for special occasions.

Serves 4
Ready in 20 minutes

- 2 medium zucchini (about 8 ounces each), sliced into thin rounds
- Fine sea salt and freshly ground black pepper
- Greek olive oil, for drizzling
- 4 halibut fillets (6 to 8 ounces each), skin removed
- 6 tablespoons basil pesto, homemade (see page 199) or store-bought
- 1 cup halved cherry tomatoes
- 12 Kalamata olives, pitted and halved
- Chopped fresh basil, for garnish
- Lemon wedges, for squeezing

1. Preheat the oven to 425°F.

2. Fold four large pieces of parchment paper in half and use scissors to cut them into wide hearts, about 18 inches in width.

3. Divide the zucchini slices among one half of each of the parchment hearts, shingling them into rectangles about the size of the fillets. Sprinkle lightly with salt and pepper and drizzle with a bit of the oil. Set the fish on the zucchini, then spread 1½ tablespoons pesto over the top of each one. Pile the tomatoes and olives on top and sprinkle lightly with salt and pepper.

4. Working with one at a time, fold the exposed parchment half over the fillets and, starting from the pointed end, twist the top and bottom parts of the paper together, going all the way around the fish until the two edges seal up the fish inside. Set them on a standard 18 by 13-inch baking sheet.

5. Transfer the pan to the oven and bake until the fish just flakes in the thickest part, 12 to 15 minutes. Remove the pan from the oven.

6. Serve hot, unwrapping the parcels at the table. Garnish with the basil and a drizzle of olive oil with lemon wedges for squeezing on the side.

Change It Up

Easy swaps: Any cooked or quick-cooking vegetable can be substituted for the zucchini: wilted greens, asparagus spears, thinly sliced onions or fennel, sliced mushrooms, or very thin potato slices. Substitute salmon, cod, or sea bass for the halibut—just start checking for doneness earlier if using thin fillets.

FÁVA
Greek Split Pea Soup

You might assume from the name that this soup features fava beans. In Greece, however, *fáva* is actually a type of split pea, and the namesake dish is a dip that's typically served as part of a mezze platter with an array of other nibbles. In my family, we've always thinned it out a bit with broth and served it as a thick, hearty soup, garnished liberally with dried oregano, capers, olives, pickled red onions, and a generous few glugs of olive oil. It's filling and has such a comforting flavor that oftentimes it's the perfect weeknight dinner, served with a salad and a stack of warm flatbreads alongside.

Serves 4 to 6
Ready in 1 hour

2¼ cups dried yellow split peas (about 1 pound)
5 tablespoons Greek olive oil, plus more for drizzling
1 large sweet onion, diced
1 medium sweet potato (about 14 ounces), peeled and cut into 2-inch chunks
4 cups low-sodium chicken or vegetable broth
3 cups water
1 teaspoon fine sea salt, plus more as needed
Dried oregano, for garnish
Capers, for serving
Kalamata olives, for serving
Favorite Pickled Red Onions (recipe follows), for serving

1. Put the split peas in a fine-mesh sieve and, standing at the sink, pour boiling water over them, allowing the water to drain off. Set the sieve over a bowl and let stand for 20 minutes.

2. Preheat a soup pot over medium heat until hot. Swirl in 1 tablespoon of the oil. Add the onion and sauté until it begins to soften, about 3 minutes. Add the sweet potato, broth, water, 1 teaspoon salt, and the drained split peas. Bring to a boil. Turn down the heat to a simmer, cover, and cook for 10 minutes. Uncover the pot and continue cooking until the split peas are tender, 15 to 20 minutes more, stirring periodically to keep them from sticking to the bottom of the pot and skimming off any foam from the surface. Taste and add additional salt as needed.

3. Remove the pot from the heat and add the remaining 4 tablespoons oil. Use an immersion blender (or working in batches in a countertop blender) to puree the soup until smooth.

4. To serve, divide among bowls and drizzle liberally with more oil. Garnish with pinches of oregano and serve with the capers, olives, and pickled red onions.

FAVORITE PICKLED RED ONIONS
Makes about 2 cups

1 cup white wine vinegar
2½ to 3½ tablespoons granulated sugar
1 tablespoon fine sea salt
1 teaspoon black peppercorns
1 medium red onion, very thinly sliced

1. In a small pot, combine the vinegar, sugar to taste, and salt and set over high heat, stirring to dissolve the sugar and watching just until steam begins to collect on the surface—don't let the mixture come to a boil.

2. Put the sliced onions in a 16-ounce or other medium-size jar or heatproof container. Pour the liquid over the onions and leave uncovered to cool to room temperature, about 1 hour.

3. Seal the jar or container and store in the refrigerator for up to 3 weeks. These are best eaten after at least 1 day of pickling in the refrigerator.

Change It Up

Easy swaps: Carrots are a great alternative to sweet potatoes here.

ARAKAS
Braised Sweet Peas with Artichokes & Chickpeas

Traditionally arakas is a dish of sweet peas that's rich with olive oil, and sometimes there are a few other vegetables mixed in. It can be served hot, warm, or even room temperature, developing additional flavor as it sits. It was a classic recipe from my yiayia's repertoire, and I grew up eating arakas all the time. I've built a bit more protein into my version by incorporating chickpeas, and the wonderful flavor and texture of artichokes give it a bit more substance. Traditionally feta would be served alongside, but I mix it in to make the dish even creamier than it already is.

Serves 4
Ready in 30 minutes

½ cup Greek olive oil, plus more for drizzling
1 small sweet onion, diced
1 large carrot, diced
4 garlic cloves, minced
2 tablespoons tomato paste
12 ounces frozen sweet peas
12 ounces frozen artichoke hearts
1 (15-ounce) can chickpeas, drained and rinsed
Fine sea salt
¼ cup chopped fresh dill
¼ cup chopped fresh parsley
1 cup vegetable broth or water
4 ounces Greek feta cheese, crumbled (about 1 cup)
Lemon wedges, for squeezing
Freshly ground black pepper, for garnish

1. Preheat a large pot or Dutch oven over medium heat until hot. Pour in the oil. Add the onion and carrot and sauté until the vegetables begin to soften, 5 to 7 minutes. Stir in the garlic, followed by the tomato paste, until it evenly coats all the vegetables.

2. Add the peas, artichokes, chickpeas, 1 teaspoon salt, dill, and parsley and toss to coat. Pour in the broth and gently stir. Cover the pot and cook until the vegetables are tender, 10 to 15 minutes, stirring occasionally.

3. Remove the pot from the heat and stir in the feta. Taste and add additional salt as needed.

4. Serve hot or warm, garnished with a drizzle of olive oil and plenty of black pepper, with lemon wedges for squeezing on the side.

Change It Up

Easy swaps: Substitute 3 medium Yukon gold potatoes, peeled and cut into bite-size chunks, for the artichokes.

AVGOLEMONO
Lemony Chicken Soup

FAN FAVORITE

This is an iconic dish in Greek cuisine, and it's what my mom and my yiayia would make for me whenever I was sick. But with a short, simple ingredient list and so much flavor and nourishment in each spoonful, it's an anytime soup to enjoy year-round. It's unique for a few reasons. First, avgolemono does not joke around with the lemon—the citrus is forthright, not a subtle back note. Second, the silky richness comes not from adding cream to the soup but by whisking tempered eggs into the broth; this requires your attention but isn't a complicated process. Even though it's traditionally made with rice, in my family and at all my favorite Greek restaurants, orzo is always the starchy component.

Serves 4
Ready in 50 minutes

- 1½ pounds boneless, skinless chicken thighs (see Note)
- 4 cups low-sodium chicken broth
- 5 cups, plus 1 tablespoon water
- 2 teaspoons fine sea salt, plus more as needed
- ¼ teaspoon freshly ground black pepper, plus more for garnish
- 1 cup orzo
- 2 large eggs
- ⅓ cup fresh lemon juice (about 3 small lemons)
- Grated lemon zest, for garnish
- Chopped fresh dill, for garnish
- Crusty bread, for serving

Note: No need to trim off the fat from the chicken thighs—it enriches the soup! And for a milder lemon flavor, feel free to scale back on the lemon juice.

1. In a large soup pot, combine the chicken, broth, and 5 cups water. Cover and bring to a boil. Add the salt and pepper, turn down the heat to low, and simmer gently, periodically peeking in to skim off any foam from the surface of the water, until the chicken is just cooked through, about 15 minutes.

2. Using tongs or a slotted spoon, transfer the cooked chicken pieces to a cutting board (don't toss the liquid!). When cool enough to handle, cut the chicken into bite-size pieces and return to the pot.

3. Return the soup to a simmer and stir in the orzo. Cover and cook for 10 minutes, stirring occasionally. Uncover, increase the heat to medium, and continue cooking until the orzo is tender, another 15 minutes. Taste the broth, adding more salt if needed. Remove the pot from the heat.

4. Crack the eggs into a large measuring cup or bowl (at least 1 quart in capacity). Add 1 tablespoon water and whisk well for about 30 seconds. Whisk in the lemon juice. Whisking constantly, slowly stream in about 2 cups of the hot broth, taking care to add it bit by bit so that you don't curdle the eggs.

5. Whisk the warmed lemon sauce into the soup pot until it's fully incorporated and silky smooth.

6. Serve immediately, garnished with the lemon zest, dill, and pepper. Serve with crusty bread. Leftover soup will keep for up to 2 days. Warm it over low heat—do not bring to a boil or else the soup will curdle.

Change It Up

Make it gluten-free: Substitute white rice for the orzo.

Lemony Greek Veal Soup: Substitute 1½ pounds veal stew meat for the chicken thighs.

LAZY SPANAKOPITA

When my mom makes spanakopita, it's a two-day affair and a labor of love, with mounds of freshly washed spinach leaves that require air-drying overnight on the countertop and the whole operation of homemade phyllo dough. But for weeknights that are short on time, I'm more inclined to this low-effort alternative that has all of spanokopita's comforting, savory flavors but none of the laborious assembly. It's one of my most popular Hungry Happens recipes, originally called Spinach & Feta Brownies. Easy and cheesy, there are rarely leftovers when I make it.

Serves 12
Ready in 1 hour

- 2 teaspoons Greek olive oil, plus more for greasing the baking dish
- 1 bunch of scallions (4 or 5), green and white parts, thinly sliced
- 10 cups baby spinach (10 ounces), coarsely chopped
- 1 cup all-purpose flour
- 1 teaspoon baking powder
- 1 teaspoon fine sea salt
- 1 cup whole milk
- 2 large eggs
- ¼ cup (4 tablespoons) melted unsalted butter, or Greek olive oil
- 2 tablespoons chopped fresh dill
- 4 ounces shredded mozzarella cheese (about 1 cup)
- 4 ounces Greek feta cheese, crumbled (about 1 cup)
- 2 tablespoons grated Parmesan cheese

1. Preheat the oven to 375°F. Lightly brush an 8 by 8-inch baking dish or other shallow 2-quart dish with olive oil.

2. Preheat a large deep pan such as a braiser over medium heat until hot. Swirl in 1 teaspoon of the oil. Add the scallions and cook just until softened, 1 to 2 minutes. Pile in half of the spinach and sauté until it's just wilted. Remove the spinach to a colander to drain and pat dry with paper towels to remove excess liquid.

3. Return the pan to the heat, swirl in the remaining 1 teaspoon oil and repeat the process of wilting and draining the remaining spinach.

4. In a large bowl, whisk together the flour, baking powder, and salt. Add the milk, eggs, and melted butter and stir just until combined. Fold in all the drained spinach, the dill, mozzarella, and feta. Spread the mixture evenly in the prepared baking dish and sprinkle with the Parmesan.

5. Transfer the dish to the oven and bake until golden brown and set in the center, 40 to 45 minutes.

6. Remove the dish from the oven and allow to cool for at least 15 minutes before slicing into twelve bars.

7. Serve warm, at room temperature, or cold. Packed in an airtight container, the bars will keep for up to 4 days in the refrigerator or for 1 month in the freezer.

Change It Up
Make it gluten-free: Substitute 1 cup superfine almond flour or oat flour for the all-purpose flour.

BROCCOLI KALTSOUNIA
Broccoli Hand Pies

We ate these veggie-stuffed hand pies a lot when I was growing up. In Greece, they're traditionally made with spinach, scallions, feta, and dill, but Mom had the idea to use broccoli, which adds a different flavor and makes them a bit more substantial. Kaltsounia are best when the filling is wrapped up in a very thin crust of dough all around, without any doughy, overlapping parts. This ensures a crunchy-soft texture when they're pan-fried and helps the pies cook evenly. It takes a bit of practice, but I find kitchen shears to be a big help, as you can see in the photos on page 128 and directions below.

Makes 6 to 8 hand pies
Ready in 1 hour 20 minutes

Dough
- 2¼ cups all-purpose flour
- 1½ teaspoons granulated sugar
- 1 teaspoon fine sea salt
- ½ teaspoon instant yeast
- ⅔ cup warm water
- ¼ cup Greek olive oil, plus more for coating
- 2 tablespoons whole milk Greek yogurt or sour cream

Filling
- 3 tablespoons Greek olive oil
- 12 ounces broccoli florets, chopped into small pieces
- ½ teaspoon fine sea salt
- ½ teaspoon red chile flakes
- 4 scallions, green and white parts, thinly sliced
- ⅓ cup coarsely chopped fresh dill, plus more for garnish
- ¼ cup coarsely chopped fresh parsley, plus more for garnish
- 4 ounces Greek feta cheese, crumbled (about 1 cup)
- 4 ounces shredded mozzarella cheese (about 1 cup)

1. To make the dough: In a bowl, whisk together the flour, sugar, salt, and yeast. Make a well in the center and pour in the water, oil, and yogurt. Use a sturdy spoon to mix until a shaggy mass forms, then tip it onto a clean work surface and knead until a smooth and soft dough forms, about 5 minutes. It will become easier to work with as you knead; you may need to add a little bit of flour to keep it from sticking but avoid adding any more than absolutely necessary. Shape into a ball, coat lightly with a bit of oil, and place the dough in a clean bowl. Cover it with a clean kitchen towel and let the dough rest for about 45 minutes.

2. To make the filling: Meanwhile, preheat a medium skillet over medium-high heat until hot. Add the oil, broccoli, salt, and chile flakes. Cook, stirring occasionally, until the broccoli is almost tender, 4 to 6 minutes. Stir in the scallions and cook until the broccoli is tender but not mushy, about 2 minutes.

3. Remove the pan from the heat, stir in the dill and parsley, and allow the mixture to cool. Once cool, stir in the feta and mozzarella.

4. To make the pies: Turn out the dough onto a clean work surface and divide into six equal portions. Working one at a time, roll out a portion as thinly as possible into a rough square shape. Roll from the center and flip and rotate the dough as you go. Scoop one-sixth of the filling into the center, leaving a 2- to 3-inch border, then stretch the exposed dough over the filling from four points. The goal is a *thin* crust around the broccoli filling, so don't overlap the excess dough; instead, pinch the seams together and trim off any excess using clean kitchen shears (see photos on page 128). Gently pat it out into an even thickness. Keep the formed pies covered with a clean kitchen towel as you fill and shape the rest of them. (You can reroll the scraps of dough into flatbreads if you like, cooking them in the same fashion as the kaltsounias below.)

(recipe continues)

To Finish
1 tablespoon Greek olive oil, plus more as needed
Chopped fresh parsley or dill, for garnish

Change It Up

Easy swaps: Substitute wilted spinach, kale, or Swiss chard for the broccoli, being sure to squeeze it dry before mixing in the scallions, herbs, and cheese.

5. To finish: Preheat a wide skillet over medium heat until hot. Swirl in the oil. Add as many pies as will fit without crowding and cook until lightly browned all over, 2 to 3 minutes per side, using tongs to crisp the edges as well if you like. Repeat to cook any remaining pies, adding more oil as needed.

6. Serve hot or warm, garnished with the parsley. Packed in an airtight container, they'll keep for up to 3 days at room temperature or for 1 month in the freezer. To reheat leftover cooked kaltsounia (thawed if necessary): Place in a dry skillet over medium-low heat and cook until crisp on the outside and heated all the way through.

LAHANOPITA STRIFTI
Spiral Pie with Cabbage & Feta

My mom's go-to vegetable pie was always spanakopita, and it appeared frequently at our table when I was growing up. It was consistently delicious, of course, but I'm someone who craves variety. So, when I make a festive Greek vegetable pie, I opt for something different like this lahanopita strifti, where a cabbage filling is rolled up into long phyllo cigars and then coiled on a baking sheet into a spiral shape. It looks stunning and has an ideal ratio of flavorful, rich filling to crispy, buttery crust.

Serves 8
Ready in 1½ hours

3 tablespoons Greek olive oil
1 medium sweet onion, diced
5 garlic cloves, finely minced
1 medium head green cabbage, shredded, or 8 cups preshredded cabbage or coleslaw mix
1 large carrot, shredded
½ teaspoon fine sea salt
Freshly ground black pepper
1 large egg
5 ounces Greek feta cheese, crumbled (about 1¼ cups)
1 small bunch of dill, coarsely chopped
6 tablespoons unsalted butter, melted
16 (9 by 14-inch) phyllo sheets (about 10 ounces), thawed overnight in the refrigerator

1. Preheat a large deep sauté pan or braiser over medium heat until hot. Swirl in the oil. Add the onion and cook just until softened but not browned, 4 to 6 minutes. Stir in the garlic. Increase the heat slightly and incrementally add a few handfuls of the cabbage and carrot—as much as will fit in an even layer. Continue adding the rest as it cooks down. Season with the salt and some pepper to taste. Cook until the cabbage is collapsed and tender, 15 to 20 minutes.

2. Remove the pan from the heat and set aside to cool for 15 to 20 minutes. Stir in the egg, feta, and dill.

3. Preheat the oven to 400°F. Line a standard 18 by 13-inch baking sheet or 12-inch cake pan with parchment paper and brush it lightly with some of the melted butter.

4. Set up an assembly station: Unroll the phyllo onto a separate baking sheet and cover it with a clean kitchen towel to prevent it from drying out. Set out a large clean and dry cutting board to work on and arrange the melted butter, the filling, and the greased baking sheet within reach.

5. Working quickly so the phyllo doesn't dry out, lay a phyllo sheet onto the board with a long side facing you and brush it lightly with butter. Set a second sheet on top and brush it lightly with butter as well. Spoon one-eighth of the filling (about ¾ cup) evenly along the bottom edge, then gently and loosely roll it up into a big cigar. Pinch the ends together and scrunch the roll up a little by gently nudging the ends together toward the center. Then carefully coil it into a spiral and set it in the center of the prepared pan. Brush it lightly with butter. Repeat this process with the remaining phyllo, creating eight rolls total, and add each one to the pan by wrapping the pieces around the center coil until you have a large circle. Brush any remaining melted butter over the top of the spirals.

6. Transfer the pan to the oven and bake until golden brown all over, 35 to 40 minutes.

7. Remove the pan from the oven and cut the pie into wedges.

8. Serve hot, warm, or at room temperature. This lahanopita strifti is best eaten within about an hour of baking it, because the light and crispy phyllo softens over time. Leftovers can be reheated in a 325°F oven for 15 to 20 minutes, until lightly crisp again.

Change It Up

Easy swaps: Filling options are limitless. Ideally you should have about 6 cups of cooked filling, and zucchini, spinach, scallions, or hearty greens like kale or Swiss chard can be used in place of, or for part of, the cabbage (they should be drained and blotted dry if necessary). Substitute mozzarella or ricotta for the feta.

LADENIA
Greek Village Pizza

Ladenia is a very old Greek bread, similar to sheet pan pizza or focaccia, that's nostalgic for me because my yiayia used to make it often when I was growing up. She'd prepare it without toppings, but traditionally, it's piled up with tomatoes, onions, and plenty of good olive oil. While you'll need to prepare the no-knead dough a day in advance so it can proof overnight in the refrigerator, the recipe requires so little hands-on time that the bread practically bakes itself, becoming fluffy, moist, and tall as it bakes in the hot oven. It's best eaten on the day it's made.

Serves 8 to 10
Ready in 18 hours

Dough
4 cups all-purpose flour
1 envelope instant yeast (2¼ teaspoons)
2 teaspoons fine sea salt
2 cups lukewarm water
2 tablespoons Greek olive oil, plus more for drizzling and greasing the pan

Topping
1½ cups diced tomatoes (8 ounces)
1 medium red onion, diced
¼ cup Greek olive oil
2 teaspoons dried oregano
1 teaspoon fine sea salt
Freshly ground black pepper

1. To make the dough: In a large bowl, stir together the flour, yeast, and salt until combined. Pour the water and oil over the mixture and stir with a sturdy spoon or spatula just until it coheres into a mass and all the flour is moistened. It will be wet. Drizzle oil lightly over the dough, cover the bowl with plastic wrap, and refrigerate overnight. The dough will double in size.

2. Liberally grease a 9 by 13-inch metal baking pan with oil. Punch down the dough to deflate it, then scrape it into the pan, gently stretching it out into an even layer. Cover loosely with plastic wrap and leave it in a warm spot in the kitchen to proof for 1 to 2 hours, until puffed up and roughly doubled in size again.

3. Preheat the oven to 400°F.

4. To prepare the topping: When you're ready to bake, in a large bowl, toss together the tomatoes, onion, oil, oregano, salt, and pepper to taste.

5. Use your fingers to dimple the dough all over into an even thickness, then spread the topping evenly on top.

6. Transfer the pan to the oven and bake until the bread is golden brown all over and cooked in the center, 40 to 50 minutes.

7. Remove the pan from the oven and slice the bread into squares.

8. Serve warm or at room temperature.

MEDITERRANEAN MEALS

5

Growing up Greek, the Mediterranean diet is a default way of eating for me. My family has always had lots of fresh vegetables and fruits in the house and has always prioritized heart-healthy fats by cooking with good olive oil and eating omega-rich proteins like fish. These recipes are some of my favorite Mediterranean meals, featuring hearty dinners that are heavily influenced by European flavors from Italy and Greece, two of my most favorite cuisines. They serve as evidence that on top of being good for you, a Mediterranean diet can be absolutely delicious, too.

SHEET PAN CHICKEN CAPONATA

Sicilian eggplant caponata is one of my favorite condiments because of its uniquely sweet-sour profile, the wonderful medley of vegetables that round out the eggplant, and the delicious, silky texture. I can eat it off a spoon. Here, an all-on-a-sheet pan version of caponata shares the stage with juicy bone-in chicken thighs that roast in the oven alongside the vegetables and lend them all their savory juices. You don't need much more than a bowl of fresh rice or crusty bread to turn it into dinner.

Serves 4 to 6
Ready in 50 minutes

3 pounds bone-in, skin-on chicken thighs
Fine sea salt and freshly ground black pepper
Italian seasoning
¼ cup Greek olive oil, plus more for drizzling
2 tablespoons red wine vinegar
2 tablespoons tomato paste
2 tablespoons honey
4 garlic cloves, minced
1 medium eggplant (about 1 pound), peeled and cut into ½-inch cubes
1 cup cherry tomatoes, halved
½ medium red onion, diced
2 celery stalks, thinly sliced
⅓ cup green olives, pitted and halved
4 dates, pitted and chopped into small pieces
2 tablespoons capers, rinsed and drained
2 tablespoons fresh lemon juice (1 medium lemon)
Chopped fresh parsley, for garnish

1. Preheat the oven to 425°F. Line a standard 18 by 13-inch sheet pan with parchment paper.

2. Blot the chicken pieces dry with paper towels and season all over with pinches of salt, pepper, and Italian seasoning.

3. In a bowl, whisk together the oil, vinegar, tomato paste, honey, garlic, 1 teaspoon Italian seasoning, ½ teaspoon salt, and a few grinds of pepper. Add the eggplant, tomatoes, onion, celery, olives, dates, and capers and toss to evenly coat.

4. Spread out the eggplant mixture on the prepared pan. Arrange the chicken pieces evenly on top and drizzle the chicken with a bit of oil.

5. Transfer the pan to the oven and bake, gently stirring the eggplant once or twice and brushing the chicken skin with any juices in the pan, until the chicken is cooked and the skin browned and crispy, 30 to 35 minutes. To achieve darker browning on the skin, switch the oven to broil and place the pan beneath the heat source for 1 to 3 minutes, watching carefully.

6. Remove the pan from the oven, squeeze the lemon juice over the pan and stir gently to combine.

7. Serve hot or warm, with the caponata spooned over the chicken or on the side, and garnish with the parsley.

Change It Up

Easy swaps: Use a whole chicken, cut into eight pieces, or skinless or skin-on breasts in place of the thighs.

HONEY-BUTTER ORANGE ROASTED CHICKEN
with Root Vegetables

Something of a spin on the Greek classic lemon chicken, here is a comforting recipe that opts for orange as the citrus and goes in a honey-butter direction. It roasts on a colorful bed of sweet potatoes and carrots, which soak up all the rich sweet-salty juices as they turn tender and caramelized. It's a showstopper one-pan dinner—just pair it with a simple salad and some crusty fresh bread, and you've got a perfect Sunday meal.

Serves 4 to 6
Ready in 2 hours

1 whole chicken (4 to 5 pounds)
Fine sea salt
1 pound sweet potatoes (about 2 medium), peeled if desired, and cut into 1- to 2-inch chunks
1 pound carrots (4 medium-to-large), peeled if desired, and cut into 1- to 2-inch chunks
1 medium sweet onion, sliced into strips
2 tablespoons Greek olive oil
4 teaspoons paprika
Freshly ground black pepper
2 navel oranges
1 medium lemon
3 sprigs of rosemary
4 tablespoons unsalted butter, melted
2 tablespoons honey
Minced fresh rosemary or thyme leaves, for garnish

Change It Up

Easy swaps: Any root vegetable can be substituted for the sweet potatoes and carrots, such as potatoes, turnips, parsnips, or golden beets.

1. Remove the neck and giblets from inside the bird, reserving them for another use. Trim off any excess skin and pat the chicken dry with paper towels, inside and out. Generously season the bird all over with salt, inside and out. If you have time, allow it to rest for an hour on the countertop, or up to overnight, covered loosely with plastic, in the refrigerator. Pat it dry once more.

2. Preheat the oven to 425°F.

3. In a roasting pan or 18 by 13-inch sheet pan, combine the sweet potatoes, carrots, onion, oil, 2 teaspoons of the paprika, ½ teaspoon salt, and several grinds of pepper. Slice one of the oranges into eight wedges and add to the pan, then toss so that everything is evenly coated. Set the chicken on top of the vegetables.

4. Juice the remaining orange and the lemon into a small bowl or measuring glass. Insert the spent rinds into the chicken cavity, along with the rosemary sprigs. Use kitchen twine to tie the legs together and, with the breast-side up, tuck the wing tips underneath the bird.

5. To the citrus juices, whisk in the melted butter, honey, the remaining 2 teaspoons paprika, and a few grinds of pepper. Drizzle and brush the mixture all over the outside of the chicken and pour the excess over the vegetables.

6. Transfer the pan to the oven and roast, stirring the vegetables and basting the bird every 20 minutes, until the juices run clear when pierced between a leg and a thigh, or an instant-read thermometer reaches 165°F, about 1½ hours. If the skin appears to be darkening too much, cover the bird with aluminum foil.

7. Remove the pan from the oven and let the chicken rest for 15 minutes before carving.

8. Serve, garnished with the minced herbs, with the vegetables on the side.

SPICY POACHED SALMON

My dad was a very healthy eater, despite—or perhaps because of—working as a baker and spending most of his days at the diners our family owned. He often opted for lean proteins like fish and chicken breasts and always wanted lots of vegetables, too. As you can tell, it was hugely influential on me! This poached salmon is a dish my mom made for him frequently. The fish is always soft and tender, never overcooked, and I always smile at the colorful variety of vegetables, channeling my dad as I cook, feeling grateful for such a dose of nourishment.

Serves 4
Ready in 30 minutes

4 tablespoons Greek olive oil
8 asparagus spears, trimmed and cut crosswise into thirds
1 large zucchini (about 12 ounces), cut into sticks 2 to 3 inches long
1 large sweet potato (about 12 ounces), peeled and sliced into ½-inch-thick half-moons
1 small jalapeño, seeded and sliced into rounds
1 teaspoon plus ¼ teaspoon fine sea salt
3 garlic cloves, minced
2 cups low-sodium chicken broth, plus more as needed
1 bay leaf
4 salmon fillets (6 ounces each)
Grated zest of ½ lemon
Juice of 1 lemon
2 tablespoons chopped fresh parsley
1 tablespoon capers, rinsed and drained
Freshly ground black pepper, for garnish

1. Preheat a wide and deep sauté pan or braiser (with a lid, and ideally nonstick) over medium heat until hot. Add 2 tablespoons of the oil, followed by the asparagus, zucchini, sweet potato, and jalapeño. Sauté until the vegetables are crisp-tender, about 3 minutes. Stir in 1 teaspoon salt and the garlic, then pour in the broth, add the bay leaf, and bring the mixture to a boil. Turn down the heat to a simmer, cover, and cook until the vegetables are tender, about 10 minutes.

2. Arrange the fish on top of the vegetables (the liquid should come only about one-quarter of the way up the height of the fish; add a bit more broth or water if necessary). Cover the pan and cook until the fish gently flakes in the center when pressed, about 5 minutes.

3. In a small bowl, whisk together the remaining 2 tablespoons oil, the lemon zest and juice, parsley, capers, and ¼ teaspoon salt.

4. Pick out the bay leaf, then divide the fish and vegetables among serving plates and spoon the sauce on top. Garnish with pepper and serve hot or warm.

Note: If you don't have a lid for your pan, a baking sheet works great as a makeshift one.

ONE-PAN CHICKEN ORZO
with Sun-Dried Tomatoes & Mozzarella

This easy, creamy, one-pan chicken dinner levels up an average Tuesday night supper. My recipe tester, Julie Bishop, described it as Mediterranean chicken biryani, which is so apt! The orzo plumps up with all the flavorful juices in the pan, making the dish thick and scoopable like a pasta bake but with no need to turn on the oven. Given my eternal love of cheese, I can't help but top the dish with fresh mozzarella—but if you'd like to make this dish dairy-free, you can leave out the cheese, and it will still be delicious.

Serves 4
Ready in 45 minutes

- 1½ pounds boneless, skinless chicken breasts, cut into strips and patted dry
- 3 tablespoons Greek olive oil
- 1½ teaspoons paprika
- 1½ teaspoons Italian seasoning
- ¼ teaspoon red chile flakes
- Fine sea salt
- 1 medium shallot, sliced into thin strips
- 2 garlic cloves, minced
- ¼ cup oil-packed sun-dried tomatoes, drained and thinly sliced
- 1 cup orzo
- 3 cups low-sodium chicken broth
- ½ cup freshly grated Parmesan cheese
- 2 cups baby spinach (2 ounces)
- 6 ounces fresh mozzarella cheese, sliced
- Chopped fresh basil, for garnish
- Freshly ground black pepper, for garnish

1. In a bowl, combine the chicken with 1 tablespoon of the oil, the paprika, Italian seasoning, chile flakes, and a few pinches of salt to taste, and toss to evenly coat.

2. Preheat a deep sauté pan or braiser over medium-high heat until hot. Swirl in 1 tablespoon of the oil. Add the chicken and cook until lightly browned all over, 2 to 3 minutes per side. Set the chicken aside on a plate.

3. Add the remaining 1 tablespoon oil to the pan, followed by the shallot. Sauté just until softened, 1 to 2 minutes. Stir in the garlic and sun-dried tomatoes. Add the orzo and stir constantly for 1 minute until it turns a light golden color. Pour in the broth and scrape up any stuck bits from the bottom, then return the chicken to the pan. Bring to a boil. Turn down the heat, cover, and simmer until the orzo is tender, 8 to 12 minutes, stirring frequently to keep it from sticking to the pan.

4. Remove the pan from the heat and stir in the Parmesan and spinach. Taste for seasoning, adding more salt if needed. Arrange the mozzarella over the top and cover the pan for a few minutes to melt the cheese.

5. Serve immediately, garnished with the basil and pepper.

CREAMY SHEET PAN GNOCCHI

Cooking store-bought, packaged gnocchi on a sheet pan is brilliant. While you'd traditionally boil them, making them soft and tender in the process, in the oven gnocchi become a little bit seared and crispy on the outside, turning them into sturdy little nuggets that are filling and substantial. In addition to a medley of vegetables, I also fold in good fresh ricotta and a few spoonfuls of pesto at the end, creating a rich, effortlessly quick sauce that bridges all the bold Italian flavors.

Serves 4
Ready in 45 minutes

1 pound shelf-stable or refrigerated gnocchi
1 pint cherry tomatoes, halved
1 red or orange bell pepper, cut into small chunks
12 ounces cremini mushrooms, quartered
½ medium red onion, cut into strips
5 garlic cloves, minced
¼ cup Greek olive oil
1 teaspoon Italian seasoning
½ teaspoon fine sea salt
Freshly ground black pepper
2 cups baby spinach (2 ounces)
½ cup good-quality ricotta cheese
2 tablespoons basil pesto, homemade (see page 199) or store-bought
Chopped fresh basil, for garnish
Freshly grated Parmesan cheese, for garnish

1. Preheat the oven to 425°F. Line a standard 18 by 13-inch sheet pan with parchment paper.

2. In a bowl, combine the gnocchi, tomatoes, bell pepper, mushrooms, onion, garlic, oil, Italian seasoning, salt, and a few grinds of pepper, tossing until evenly coated. Spread out the mixture on the prepared pan.

3. Transfer the pan to the oven and bake until the tomatoes have become saucy, about 30 minutes.

4. Spread the spinach over the mixture and return the pan to the oven until it wilts, 3 to 5 minutes more.

5. Remove the pan from the oven and stir to distribute the spinach into the gnocchi. Dollop with the ricotta and pesto and gently stir to combine.

6. Serve hot, garnished with the basil and Parmesan.

Change It Up

Easy swaps: Break two balls of Burrata cheese over the pasta in place of the ricotta.

LEMONY ORZOTTO
with Spinach & Peas

Combining my love of risotto with the enjoyment I get out of putting spins on traditional recipes, I came up with this less involved but equally delicious orzo recipe. Orzotto is simply risotto made using orzo instead of rice. It's creamy and comforting, and this one is bright and fresh, too, with a prominent lemony flavor and a good dose of greens. I find it to be a perfect springtime dish, in part because it's also a great way to showcase produce like asparagus, snap peas, and other tender spring vegetables if you'd like to change things up. It works as a vegetarian main or as a side dish for roasted or grilled meats.

Serves 4
Ready in 30 minutes

2 tablespoons Greek olive oil
½ medium sweet onion, diced
1 long celery stalk, diced
1 teaspoon red chile flakes
Fine sea salt
3 garlic cloves, finely minced
1½ cups orzo
3 cups low-sodium vegetable or chicken broth
1 cup fresh or frozen sweet peas (unthawed if frozen)
5 cups baby spinach (5 ounces)
1 cup freshly grated Parmesan cheese, plus more for garnish
1 tablespoon unsalted butter
Grated zest and juice of 1 lemon, plus more as needed
Chopped fresh parsley, for garnish
Freshly ground black pepper, for garnish

1. Preheat a deep sauté pan or braiser over medium heat until hot. Swirl in the oil. Add the onion, celery, chile flakes, and ½ teaspoon salt and sauté until the vegetables are soft and translucent, 5 to 7 minutes. Stir in the garlic and cook until fragrant. Add the orzo and broth and bring to a gentle boil. Turn down the heat to a simmer, partially cover, and cook until the orzo is tender, stirring occasionally to prevent it from sticking to the sides or bottom of the pot, 10 to 12 minutes.

2. Stir in the peas and add the spinach incrementally, as it wilts into the pasta. Finally, add the Parmesan, butter, lemon zest and juice and stir vigorously to incorporate. Season with more salt or lemon juice to taste.

3. Serve hot, garnished with the parsley, pepper, and more Parmesan.

Note: The orzotto will thicken and solidify as it cools; to make it creamy again, stir in a few splashes of broth or water as you reheat it.

Change It Up

Easy swaps: Substitute asparagus or carrots, cut into thin rounds or a small dice, or fresh or frozen corn kernels for the peas. Substitute Greek feta for the Parmesan and garnish the dish with dill at the end.

EPIC MEAT LASAGNA

This recipe has been in our family for years, and my son, Yiannis, asks for it by exactly this name: "that epic meat lasagna." It's a recipe that has a few extra steps, but the outcome is so worth the effort. If I'm making it for a family dinner, I use cottage cheese in the filling; this produces a slightly lighter version. But if I'm making it for a party, I use the more traditional and richer ricotta cheese. It's important not to slice into the baked lasagna too soon or else the slices will not come out clean and neat. Give it at least 15 or even 30 minutes to rest. The flavors are even better the next day.

Serves 6
Ready in 1½ hours

Meat Sauce
1 tablespoon Greek olive oil
1 medium sweet onion, diced
4 garlic cloves, minced
2 tablespoons tomato paste
½ teaspoon dried oregano
¼ teaspoon red chile flakes
1 teaspoon fine sea salt
Freshly ground black pepper
1 pound ground beef (95/5)
½ pound ground pork
1 (28-ounce) can crushed tomatoes
1 (28-ounce) can diced tomatoes
3 tablespoons light brown sugar
¼ cup fresh basil leaves

Filling
2 cups whole milk cottage cheese or good quality ricotta (16 ounces), drained
¼ cup fine dried bread crumbs
1½ cups coarsely shredded mozzarella cheese (6 ounces)
½ cup shredded Parmesan cheese
½ cup fresh basil leaves
1 large egg
¼ teaspoon ground nutmeg
¼ teaspoon fine sea salt
Freshly ground black pepper

Assembly
12 dry lasagna noodles (regular or no-boil)
1½ cups coarsely shredded mozzarella cheese (6 ounces)
Chopped fresh basil, for garnish
Red chile flakes, for garnish

1. To make the meat sauce: Preheat a large pot over medium heat until hot. Swirl in the oil. Add the onion and sauté until translucent, 4 to 5 minutes. Stir in the garlic, tomato paste, oregano, chile flakes, salt, and pepper to taste. Add the ground beef and pork and, using a wooden spoon, break apart the meat into crumbles and cook until it's no longer pink. Stir in the tomatoes and brown sugar. Lower the heat to achieve a simmer and cook, uncovered, stirring occasionally, until the sauce thickens slightly, 15 to 20 minutes. Taste and adjust the seasoning as needed. Remove the pot from the heat and stir in the basil. Cover the pot and set aside.

2. To make the filling: In a food processor, combine the cottage cheese, bread crumbs, mozzarella, Parmesan, basil, egg, nutmeg, salt, and pepper to taste. Pulse until mostly smooth.

3. Preheat the oven to 375°F.

4. To assemble: Spoon 1½ cups of the meat sauce evenly over the bottom of a 9 by 13-inch baking dish. Lay three lasagna noodles over the sauce and top them with one-third of the filling mixture and a few extra spoonfuls of the sauce so the noodles are fully moistened. Repeat this process three more times to create a total of four layers of lasagna. Pour all the remaining sauce over the top layer of noodles and sprinkle with the mozzarella. Cover the baking dish with parchment paper and then aluminum foil, sealing it tightly.

5. Transfer the baking dish to the oven and bake for 35 minutes. Uncover the pan and continue baking until the top is golden brown, another 15 minutes or so.

6. Remove the pan from the oven and let cool for at least 15 minutes before slicing.

7. To serve, garnish with the basil and chile flakes.

BROCCOLI-FETA PASTA BAKE

Here, the viral TikTok baked feta pasta gets a Hungry Happens twist. I've opted to feature fiber-rich and super-flavorful roasted broccoli, one of my favorite vegetables and an incredible pairing for feta cheese. The broccoli and cheese roast together, along with olives and garlic; that will become the sauce. Finally, cooked pasta is added straight to the pan, and everything is combined, turning rich and creamy. It's such an easy vegetarian dinner and always so hearty and comforting.

Serves 4
Ready in 40 minutes

1 pound broccoli, florets and stalks chopped into small pieces (about 5 cups)
½ cup pitted Kalamata olives, halved
3 large garlic cloves, minced
⅓ cup Greek olive oil, plus more for drizzling
Fine sea salt
Red chile flakes
1 (7- to 8-ounce) block Greek feta cheese
10 ounces (about 2¾ cups) medium-size pasta (see Note)
Sliced or torn fresh basil, for garnish
Grated lemon zest, for garnish

1. Preheat the oven to 400°F.

2. In a 9 by 13-inch baking dish, combine the broccoli, olives, garlic, oil, and a few pinches of both salt and chile flakes and toss until evenly coated. Clear a space in the middle of the pan and set the block of feta in it. Drizzle the cheese with a bit more oil and another pinch or two of chile flakes.

3. Transfer the pan to the oven and bake for 15 minutes. Increase the oven temperature to 425°F and bake for another 20 minutes.

4. Meanwhile, bring a large saucepan of salted water to a boil. Add the pasta and cook to al dente, according to the package directions. Reserving about ½ cup of the cooking water, drain the pasta.

5. Once the broccoli is done, remove the pan from the oven and immediately mix the cheese into the roasted vegetables, using a spatula or wooden spoon. Add the cooked pasta along with the reserved pasta water and stir to combine.

6. Serve hot, garnished with the basil and lemon zest.

Note: A medium-size pasta shape, such as farfalle, fusilli, penne, or gemelli, works best.

Change It Up

Easy swaps: Halved Brussels sprouts, cauliflower florets, or green beans can be substituted for the broccoli.

Amp it up: Add cubes of chicken breast or chicken tenders to the pan to roast along with the vegetables and cheese.

SMOKY SPANISH LENTIL SOUP
with Chorizo

This hearty, fragrant soup tastes as if it spent hours simmering on the stove, but it's actually a pretty quick, one-pot affair that's perfectly suitable for weeknights. Chorizo provides so much richness and sweet, spicy flavor, and I've added extra layers of deliciousness with paprika, tomato paste, and fire-roasted tomatoes (which I love in soups like this, for the lightly charred flavor). And as a fiber boost, there's a healthy dose of lentils in there, too. With any kind of soup that includes beans or lentils, it's so important not to be shy with salt—season liberally, as it makes all the difference.

Serves 6
Ready in 50 minutes

1 tablespoon Greek olive oil, plus more for drizzling
12 ounces Spanish chorizo, casings removed and torn into crumbles
1 medium sweet onion, diced
2 medium carrots, sliced into ¼-inch rounds
2 celery stalks, sliced
4 garlic cloves, minced
2 tablespoons tomato paste
1 teaspoon paprika
4 cups low-sodium chicken broth
2 cups water
1 (14.5-ounce) can diced tomatoes, preferably fire-roasted
1 cup brown lentils, sorted through and rinsed
Fine sea salt and freshly ground black pepper
2 cups baby spinach (2 ounces)
Red wine vinegar
Chopped fresh parsley, for garnish

1. Preheat a soup pot over medium-high heat, then swirl in the oil. Add the chorizo and cook until browned and a bit crispy, 7 to 9 minutes.

2. Add the onion, carrots, and celery and sauté until softened, 6 to 8 minutes. Stir in the garlic, tomato paste, and paprika. Stir again to ensure the vegetables are well coated in the tomato paste, then add the broth, water, tomatoes, lentils, 1 teaspoon salt, and pepper to taste. Bring to a boil. Turn down the heat to a simmer and cook, uncovered, until the lentils are soft and tender, 20 to 25 minutes.

3. Just before serving, add the spinach and stir until it wilts, followed by a splash of vinegar. Taste, and add additional salt or vinegar as needed.

4. To serve, garnish each bowl with a drizzle of oil and a sprinkling of parsley.

CRUNCHY POTATO SCHIACCIATA

Schiacciata is a thin Italian flatbread that was introduced to our family by an Italian neighbor we knew growing up, with whom we often exchanged delicious foods. My recipe takes a more vegetable-centric approach than many traditional recipes—in fact, it's composed primarily of vegetables, with only a little flour. It bakes into a tender slice that's full of savory flavor, and the cornmeal creates a delectably crisp crust (my favorite part). For the best schiacciata experience, it's important to press the mixture firmly into the pan and ensure that it's thin so it develops maximum crispiness.

Serves 8
Ready in 50 minutes

Cornmeal, for sprinkling
1½ cups peeled and coarsely grated Yukon gold potatoes (about 8 ounces)
¾ cup peeled and coarsely grated carrot (1 large)
1 medium zucchini, coarsely grated (6 to 8 ounces; about 1 cup)
1 cup all-purpose flour
½ cup coarsely grated Parmesan cheese, plus more for sprinkling
2 tablespoons Greek olive oil
½ teaspoon paprika
½ teaspoon onion powder
½ teaspoon garlic powder
½ teaspoon fine sea salt
Freshly ground black pepper
⅓ cup water
Sour cream, for serving

1. Preheat the oven to 400°F. Line a 9-inch round cake pan with parchment paper (see page 40 for my parchment-lining trick) and sprinkle the bottom with cornmeal.

2. In a bowl, combine the potatoes, carrot, zucchini, flour, Parmesan, oil, paprika, onion powder, garlic powder, salt, pepper to taste, and water. Use a sturdy spoon or spatula to mix well, until a smooth, thick batter forms.

3. Scrape the batter into the prepared pan and press it firmly and evenly to make a smooth surface. Sprinkle with more Parmesan and cornmeal.

4. Transfer the pan to the oven and bake the bread until the top is golden brown and set in the center, 45 to 50 minutes.

5. Remove the pan from the oven and let the schiacciata cool in the pan for 10 minutes, then, using the parchment, unmold it and cool on a wire rack for an additional 15 minutes.

6. Slice into wedges and serve warm, with sour cream on the side.

Note: Do not squeeze out any of the liquid from the shredded vegetables—you need it to flavor and hydrate the flour. And if you don't have cornmeal, use bread crumbs or panko instead.

Change It Up

Make it gluten-free: Substitute superfine almond flour for the all-purpose flour.

LEEK & ZUCCHINI SCARPACCIA

This thin, rustic vegetable tart is impossible to stop snacking on, with its crusty exterior and rich caramelized flavor from the cooked leeks and zucchini. I love to pair it with soups at dinnertime, but it's equally good as a midday snack or savory breakfast. Or you can cut it into bite-size squares and serve it as an appetizer at a party. Because the crispiness is so delicious, I strongly recommend using a metal baking pan rather than a glass one for the best result.

Serves 4
Ready in 45 minutes

1 large leek
2 tablespoons Greek olive oil
2 medium zucchini (6 to 8 ounces each), sliced into rounds
Fine sea salt and freshly ground black pepper
Olive oil cooking spray
⅓ cup cornmeal, plus more for sprinkling
1 cup all-purpose flour
½ teaspoon garlic powder
½ teaspoon paprika
½ teaspoon dried oregano
1 cup water
⅓ cup pitted and chopped Kalamata olives
2 tablespoons grated Parmesan cheese
Chopped fresh basil, for garnish
Red chile flakes, for garnish

1. Trim off the root and dark green parts of the leek. Slice it lengthwise down the middle, then, with the flat sides down, slice it into half-moons. Place the slices in a bowl and cover with cold water, swishing them around to dislodge any dirt. Rinse and repeat until the water runs clean, then drain and blot dry with paper towels.

2. Preheat a large deep sauté pan or braiser over medium heat until hot. Swirl in 1 tablespoon of the oil. Add the zucchini, leek, and a few pinches of salt and pepper and sauté until the vegetables are browned, 6 to 8 minutes, stirring periodically. Remove the pan from the heat and allow to cool slightly.

3. Preheat the oven to 350°F. Line a 9 by 13-inch metal baking pan with parchment paper and spray it with the cooking spray. Sprinkle some cornmeal over the bottom of the pan.

4. In a bowl, whisk together the flour, cornmeal, garlic powder, paprika, oregano, ½ teaspoon salt, and a few grinds of pepper. Add the water, olives, and the remaining 1 tablespoon oil and use a spoon or spatula to stir until a batter forms. Fold in the sautéed leek and zucchini.

5. Scrape the batter into the prepared pan and spread it out thinly and evenly. Sprinkle the top with the Parmesan and some more cornmeal, then spray it lightly with the cooking spray.

6. Transfer the pan to the oven and bake until golden brown and crispy, 45 to 50 minutes. Allow to cool for at least 15 minutes before slicing.

7. To serve, garnish with the basil and chile flakes.

HERBY RICOTTA DUMPLINGS
in Vegetable Soup

Dumplings are a great way to transform a light and brothy soup into a substantial, satisfying meal. These ricotta dumplings are related to Italian gnudi, which are made mostly from very fresh, good-quality ricotta cheese. They should be delicate and tender, so you can gently break into one with your soup spoon and eat a bite along with the rich, nourishing broth. This is a great vegetarian soup if you use vegetable broth, but I like it best with a richer and more flavorful chicken broth—in either instance, it's an excellent recipe for the best-quality or homemade broth you can get your hands on.

Serves 4
Ready in 1 hour

Dumplings
2 cups good-quality ricotta cheese (16 ounces)
2 large eggs, lightly beaten
½ cup (packed) freshly grated Parmesan cheese
½ cup finely minced fresh parsley or dill
½ teaspoon fine sea salt
Freshly ground black pepper
1 cup panko bread crumbs
¼ cup all-purpose flour, plus more for coating

Soup
3 tablespoons Greek olive oil
2 medium carrots, peeled and diced
2 celery stalks, thinly sliced
½ medium sweet onion, diced
8 ounces cremini mushrooms, sliced
3 garlic cloves, finely minced
2 bay leaves
4 cups reduced-sodium vegetable or chicken broth
Fine sea salt

4 tablespoons basil pesto, homemade (see page 199) or store-bought, for topping
Chopped fresh parsley or dill, for garnish
Lemon wedges, for squeezing

1. To make the dumplings: In a bowl, stir together the ricotta, eggs, Parmesan, parsley, salt, and a few grinds of pepper until well combined. Stir in the panko. Set the mixture aside for about 30 minutes to thicken up slightly, while you prepare the soup.

2. To make the soup: Preheat a soup pot over medium heat until hot. Swirl in the oil. Add the carrots, celery, onion, and mushrooms and cook, stirring occasionally, until the vegetables are tender and beginning to caramelize, 8 to 10 minutes.

3. Stir in the garlic, bay leaves, and broth and bring to a boil. Turn down the heat to a gentle simmer, cover, and cook until the flavors bloom, 20 to 30 minutes. Taste the soup and add salt if needed.

4. Spread the flour on a plate or in a shallow bowl. Making a few at a time, use a cookie scoop or two spoons to shape the ricotta mixture into rough balls, about 1½ tablespoons per dumpling, then drop them into the flour. Gently roll the balls in the flour so they're lightly coated all over and then shape into oblong balls about 1 inch in diameter.

5. Add as many dumplings as will fit in a single layer to the simmering broth, cover the pot, and cook until the dumplings have firmed up and cooked all the way through, 8 to 10 minutes (you can test one by removing it from the pot with a slotted spoon and cutting it in half).

6. Use a slotted spoon to scoop out the cooked dumplings and add them to soup bowls, about five per serving. (Repeat the process to cook the remaining dumplings, if necessary.) Ladle the soup over them and top each one with a spoonful of pesto.

7. Pick out the bay leaves, garnish with parsley, and serve right away with lemon wedges on the side for squeezing.

EURO TORTELLINI SALAD

A package of store-bought tortellini can be such a terrific, time-saving ingredient to keep around, because it's practically a ready-made meal. Here, tortellini are the stars of a quick, hearty salad that's bursting with plenty of texture—marinated artichoke hearts, crunchy cucumbers, mozzarella, olives, and more. The tortellini also have the advantage of soaking up the salad's bold flavors as it sits, making it a helpful one for preparing in advance and packing up for road trips and picnics; just pile the chopped spinach on top of the salad, then mix it in just before you eat. My preference is for fresh tortellini, but the shelf-stable dried ones will work in a pinch.

Serves 4
Ready in 20 minutes

Fine sea salt
1 (10-ounce) package fresh tortellini (any flavor)
1 cup cherry tomatoes, halved
2 Persian (mini) cucumbers, cubed
½ small or ¼ medium red onion, thinly sliced

Dressing
6 tablespoons Greek olive oil
3 tablespoons red wine vinegar
2 teaspoons honey or maple syrup
1 teaspoon Dijon mustard
1 garlic clove, minced
½ teaspoon dried oregano
Fine sea salt and freshly ground black pepper

Assembly
1 cup marinated artichoke hearts, drained and halved or quartered
½ cup mozzarella pearls (5 ounces) or crumbled Greek feta cheese (2 ounces)
¼ cup Kalamata olives, halved and pitted
4 ounces thinly sliced salami, cut into thin strips
1 tablespoon capers, coarsely chopped
5 cups baby spinach or other tender salad greens (5 ounces), coarsely chopped
Freshly ground black pepper, for garnish

1. Bring a large pot of salted water to a boil. Add the tortellini and cook according to the package directions, usually 5 to 7 minutes for fresh. Drain in a colander and place under cold running water until cooled.

2. Meanwhile, in a large bowl, toss together the tomatoes, cucumbers, onion, and ¼ teaspoon salt and let stand for a few minutes while the pasta cooks.

3. To make the dressing: In a screw-top jar or small bowl, combine all the ingredients and shake or whisk until combined. Taste and add more seasoning as needed.

4. To assemble: Add the cooled tortellini to the bowl with the tomatoes along with the artichokes, mozzarella, olives, salami, and capers. Add dressing to taste and toss to combine.

5. Just before serving, mix in the spinach. Garnish with pepper.

＃ CARB LIGHT

If you've been following my cooking on Instagram or TikTok, you know that I specialize in taking familiar recipes and turning them into low-carb dishes that don't sacrifice on the delicious. I see it as a challenge to get creative with veggies! I love to turn things like pizza (see pages 169 and 177) and tacos (see page 174) into healthy, low-carb meals. And approaching lean proteins like chicken breasts or fish fillets as vessels for hearty veggies (and sometimes some cheese, of course) not only makes dinner easy by combining protein and veg in the same dish, but also keeps everything balanced and satiating.

LOW-CARB CHICKEN NUGGETS
with Crispy Baked French Fries

These chicken nuggets are made with whole ingredients and good-quality chicken, so that you know exactly what's in them. Rather than a bread crumb coating, they have a crispy, cheesy crust that eliminates the carbs and tastes even better. If you add the french fries, put the nuggets in the oven at Step 4 of the fries, once the temperature is increased.

Serves 4 to 6
Ready in 45 minutes

Spicy Ketchup
¼ cup ketchup
1½ teaspoons Worcestershire sauce
1 teaspoon sriracha sauce

Chicken Nuggets
½ cup plus ⅓ cup shredded Parmesan cheese
3 tablespoons potato starch, tapioca starch, or cornstarch
½ teaspoon plus ¾ teaspoon paprika
½ teaspoon dried parsley
2 pounds ground chicken
2 large eggs
½ cup shredded mozzarella cheese
¾ teaspoon garlic powder
¾ teaspoon onion powder
2 teaspoons fine sea salt
Olive oil cooking spray, for spraying the nugget tops
Crispy Baked French Fries (recipe follows), for serving

Change It Up
Turkey Nuggets: Substitute ground turkey for the chicken.

1. Preheat the oven to 425°F. Line a standard 18 by 13-inch baking sheet with parchment paper.

2. To make the ketchup: In a small bowl, whisk together the ketchup, Worcestershire sauce, and sriracha.

3. To make the nuggets: In a shallow bowl, whisk together ½ cup of the Parmesan, the potato starch, ½ teaspoon of the paprika, and the parsley.

4. Using your hands, in a large bowl, combine the ground chicken, eggs, mozzarella, garlic powder, onion powder, salt, the remaining ⅓ cup Parmesan, and the remaining ¾ teaspoon paprika until just incorporated.

5. Scoop the mixture into balls about 1½ tablespoons each (a spring-loaded cookie scoop works great for this), then quickly dredge them in the Parmesan mixture, shape them into ovals, and arrange them in a single layer on the prepared pan. Spray the tops of the nuggets with the cooking spray.

6. Transfer the pan to the oven and bake for 15 minutes, then carefully flip each nugget. Return the pan to the oven and bake until evenly browned and firm to the touch, about 10 more minutes. Remove the pan from the oven.

7. Serve hot or warm, along with the ketchup and french fries.

CRISPY BAKED FRENCH FRIES
Serves 4

4 pounds russet potatoes (about 4 large), peeled
3 tablespoons potato starch or cornstarch
¼ cup Greek olive oil
Fine sea salt

1. Slice the potatoes into fry shapes about ½ inch in thickness. Place them in a bowl and cover with cold water. Soak for 10 minutes and up to a few hours, then drain and pat dry with paper towels.

2. When ready to bake, preheat the oven to 375°F. Line a standard 18 by 13-inch baking sheet with parchment paper.

3. In a dry bowl, toss the potatoes with the potato starch until evenly coated. Add the oil and toss again. Spread out the potatoes on the prepared pan.

4. Transfer the pan to the oven and bake until tender, about 20 minutes. Stir the fries and increase the heat to 425°F. Continue baking until the fries are nicely browned and crispy, another 10 to 20 minutes more. Sprinkle liberally with salt to taste.

VEGETABLE-STUFFED CHICKEN BREASTS

Stuffed chicken breasts are typically quite fussy, requiring that you butterfly the breasts and then wrap them around a filling, using toothpicks to hold everything in place. Here, we're just making a few cuts into the chicken breasts to make a big internal pocket that is easy to stuff full of broccoli or another favorite veggie—mushrooms, asparagus, cauliflower, and carrots all work well, as long as they're chopped small enough that they cook quickly. My family always loves these for dinner, especially when served with Crispy Baked French Fries (page 165) or a simple salad, like Yiayia's Maroulosalata (page 216).

Serves 4
Ready in 40 minutes

 GF

1 teaspoon paprika
1 teaspoon garlic powder
1 teaspoon onion powder
1 teaspoon Italian seasoning or dried oregano
1¼ teaspoons fine sea salt
3 cups chopped broccoli florets and stalks (about ½ pound)
½ red bell pepper, finely diced
1½ cups shredded Mexican cheese blend or mozzarella
4 boneless, skinless chicken breasts
2 tablespoons Greek olive oil
Chopped fresh parsley, for garnish
Red chile flakes, for garnish

Change It Up

Easy swaps: Use chopped mushrooms, asparagus, carrots, or cauliflower in place of the broccoli.

1. Preheat the oven to 350°F. Line a standard 18 by 13-inch baking sheet with parchment paper.

2. In a small bowl, combine the paprika, garlic powder, onion powder, Italian seasoning, and 1 teaspoon of the salt.

3. In a medium bowl, combine the broccoli, bell pepper, ½ cup of the cheese, and the remaining ¼ teaspoon salt.

4. Working with one chicken breast at a time, lay it flat on a cutting board and make a lengthwise cut down the middle, almost reaching the bottom but being careful not to cut all the way through it. Pry the incision open, then use your knife to slice along each inner edge of your initial cut, cutting into the breast to make a pocket on either side. This should enable you to pry the breast open and make plenty of room for filling (see step-by-step photos, below). Rub the oil all over each chicken piece, then sprinkle the seasoning blend all over. Arrange the breasts on the prepared pan.

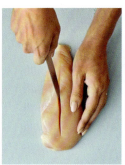  

5. Divide the broccoli mixture among the chicken pockets, piling it on if necessary. Top each piece with some of the remaining 1 cup cheese and press down gently to make the mixture more compact.

6. Transfer the pan to the oven and bake until the chicken is fully cooked and the cheese is lightly browned, 25 to 30 minutes. If you'd like, switch the oven to broil and place the pan beneath the heat source for 1 to 3 minutes, watching carefully, until the cheese is blistered. Remove the pan from the oven.

7. Serve the chicken hot, garnished with the parsley and chile flakes.

MEDITERRANEAN TURKEY-CRUST PIZZA

You may already know that I have an obsession with reinventing pizzas that are packed with veggies and are lower in carbs. This is one of those recipes, and in addition, it's made with a high-protein pizza crust. Being pizza, there is plenty of flexibility in the toppings and even in the ground meat base (see below for some of my favorite swaps). But the key is to press the crust thin, blot away the moisture that collects in the pan, and bake it on both sides. I also like to use this "crust" as a base for salad.

Serves 3 or 4
Ready in 50 minutes

Crust
1 pound ground turkey (85/15)
½ cup shredded mozzarella cheese
¼ cup grated Parmesan cheese
1 large egg
2 garlic cloves, minced
1 teaspoon Italian seasoning
¾ teaspoon fine sea salt
Freshly ground black pepper

Toppings
1 medium tomato, sliced into rounds
1 cup shredded mozzarella cheese
1 ounce Greek feta cheese, crumbled (about ¼ cup)
½ green bell pepper, thinly sliced
½ small red onion, thinly sliced
10 to 12 Kalamata olives, pitted and halved

Fresh basil leaves, for garnish

1. Preheat the oven to 425°F. Line a standard 18 by 13-inch baking sheet with parchment paper.

2. To make the crust: In a bowl, combine the turkey, mozzarella, Parmesan, egg, garlic, Italian seasoning, salt, and a few grinds of pepper.

3. Add the mixture to the prepared pan and spread it out to form a large round or oval shape. Using moistened hands, press it out as thinly as possible, aiming for a thickness of about ¼ inch. It's important for the meat to be thin so that it becomes crisp in the oven.

4. Transfer the pan to the oven and bake for 20 minutes. Remove the pan from the oven and blot the crust with paper towels to soak up any moisture that has collected on the surface. Carefully flip the crust over (see Note), return the pan to the oven, and bake until the edges are golden brown, about 20 minutes more.

5. To add the toppings: Remove the pan from the oven and arrange all the toppings evenly over the crust. Switch the oven to broil and place the pan beneath the heat source until the toppings are lightly browned and the cheese has melted, 3 to 5 minutes, watching carefully so that it doesn't burn.

6. Remove the pan from the oven and garnish with the basil leaves.

7. Slice and serve hot or warm.

Change It Up

Easy swaps: Use ground chicken, ground beef, or ground pork instead of the turkey, but note that fattier meats will release more liquid and will need to be blotted periodically during baking.

Note: To easily flip the crust, lay a sheet of parchment over it, then set a clean cutting board or baking sheet on top. Wearing oven mitts, flip the pan over. Then, using the parchment that's now on the bottom, slide the crust back onto the pan.

SPINACH & FETA STUFFED SALMON

Salmon fillets are a real staple of busy weeknights at my house, since they cook so quickly and are rich in healthful fats, nutrients, and protein. These stuffed fillets take only a few minutes of extra effort, and they get something of a Greek-ified spin from seasoned spinach and creamy, tangy feta tucked inside a little pocket in the fish. There are a couple of tricks here: First, take care not to overcook the spinach or else it turns the filling watery. And second, my secret for cooking beautiful salmon is to let it come to room temperature for 30 minutes before putting it in the oven—this helps prevent the white, gunky stuff (a protein called albumin) from forming.

Serves 4
Ready in 30 minutes

- 4 salmon fillets (6 ounces each), rinsed and patted dry
- 2 tablespoons Greek olive oil
- 3 scallions, green and white parts, thinly sliced
- 1 garlic clove, minced
- 4 cups baby spinach (4 ounces)
- 1 tablespoon chopped fresh dill
- Fine sea salt and freshly ground black pepper
- 3 ounces Greek feta cheese, crumbled (about ¾ cup)
- Paprika, for dusting

1. About 30 minutes prior to baking, remove the salmon from the refrigerator to let it come to room temperature.

2. Preheat the oven to 425°F. Line a standard 18 by 13-inch sheet pan with parchment paper.

3. Set the fillets on their sides on the baking sheet. Using a sharp paring knife, cut "pockets" into the salmon by carefully slicing into the thickest part, parallel to the skin but taking care not to cut all the way through. Gently pry each pocket open so you can tuck filling inside.

4. Preheat a skillet over medium-high heat until hot. Add 1 tablespoon of the oil and the scallions and sauté until just softened, 1 to 2 minutes. Stir in the garlic. Add the spinach, dill, and a few pinches of salt and pepper to taste. Sauté until the spinach is mostly wilted but not entirely, then transfer the mixture immediately to a bowl. Allow to cool for 5 minutes, then mix in the feta.

5. Carefully divide the mixture among the salmon pockets. Turn them skin-side down and brush the tops and sides of the fish with the remaining 1 tablespoon oil. Sprinkle evenly with salt and pepper and dust with a bit of paprika.

6. Transfer the pan to the oven and bake until the fish is just firm to the touch and an instant-read thermometer reaches 125°F, 14 to 17 minutes.

7. Remove the pan from the oven and serve immediately.

Change It Up

Easy swaps: Substitute your favorite green, such as Swiss chard or kale, for the spinach. Just be sure to adjust the cooking time as needed, since heartier greens will require more time to wilt.

SEASIDE TUNA TOSTADAS

Tuna tostadas are always a refreshing, satisfying dish to order at a Mexican restaurant, but they're simple to make at home, too, assuming you can get your hands on good-quality, sashimi-grade tuna that's safe to eat raw. (If you don't like to eat raw fish, you can substitute cooked shrimp, flaked cooked salmon, or even good-quality canned tuna instead.) While there is room to improvise, make sure to go bold with flavors and textures. Here, we've got a crunchy tostada; creamy avocado; cool, fresh fish; spicy and rich mayonnaise—and a final garnish of crispy shallots that take the tostadas to the next level.

Serves 4
Ready in 40 minutes

4 medium or 8 small corn tortillas
Olive oil cooking spray, for spraying the tortillas
Fine sea salt

Spicy Mayo Sauce
½ cup mayonnaise, preferably Kewpie
Juice of 1 lime
2 teaspoons sriracha sauce, plus more as needed
½ teaspoon honey

Toppings
8 ounces sashimi-grade tuna, cut into small cubes
1 medium cucumber, peeled, seeded, and diced
¼ red onion, diced
1 jalapeño, diced (seeded if desired)
Juice of 1 lime, plus more as needed
Fine sea salt
1 avocado
Thinly sliced scallion, for garnish
Toasted sesame seeds, for garnish
Crispy Shallots (page 212), for garnish

1. Preheat the oven to 325°F. Line a standard 18 by 13-inch baking sheet with parchment paper.

2. Arrange the tortillas in a single layer on the pan. Spray them evenly but lightly on both sides with the cooking spray.

3. Transfer the pan to the oven and bake for about 10 minutes, then flip each tortilla over and continue baking until they're crisp, another 5 to 10 minutes. Right out of the oven, sprinkle them lightly with salt, then set aside to cool.

4. To make the sauce: In a small bowl, stir together the mayonnaise, lime juice, sriracha, and honey. Taste, and add more sriracha if needed.

5. To prepare the toppings: In a bowl, combine the tuna, cucumber, onion, jalapeño, the juice of 1 lime, and a few pinches of salt. Taste and add more lime and/or salt if needed.

6. In a small bowl, coarsely mash the avocado with a few pinches of salt.

7. Spread each tortilla with a scoop of the mashed avocado, then spoon the tuna mixture on top. Garnish with the scallion, sesame seeds, and crispy shallots. Drizzle with the sauce and serve right away.

CHILI-LIME SHRIMP "TACOS"
with Pineapple Salsa

My family loves taco night—who doesn't? It's a healthy dinner that's quick to throw together and so easy for everyone to assemble however they please, with lots of fun fillings and garnishes to go around. We sometimes like to swap out the tortillas for big crunchy romaine leaves. This gives the tacos a fresher, lower-carb, more salad-y vibe, and with the fruity, spicy pineapple salsa, these are a perfect summer meal. Instead of lettuce cups, you can serve this with rice to make a bowl or go the traditional route and use corn or flour tortillas.

Makes 8 tacos
Ready in 30 minutes

Pineapple Salsa
1 cup diced fresh pineapple
1 avocado, finely diced
½ red bell pepper, finely diced
¼ red onion, finely diced
1 small jalapeño, finely diced
2 tablespoons chopped fresh cilantro
1 tablespoon Greek olive oil
Grated zest and juice of ½ lime
½ teaspoon Tajín seasoning (optional)
Fine sea salt and freshly ground black pepper

Lime Crema
½ cup whole milk Greek yogurt or sour cream
Grated zest and juice of ½ lime
½ teaspoon honey

Shrimp
24 peeled and deveined wild shrimp (about 1¼ pounds), dried thoroughly
2 tablespoons Greek olive oil
¾ teaspoon garlic powder
¾ teaspoon onion powder
¾ teaspoon chili powder
¾ teaspoon paprika
½ teaspoon fine sea salt
¼ teaspoon ground cumin
⅛ teaspoon freshly ground black pepper
Juice of 1 lime

Assembly
8 large romaine lettuce leaves
Toasted sesame seeds, for garnish
Tajín seasoning, for garnish (optional)
Fresh cilantro leaves, for garnish
Favorite Pickled Red Onions (page 119), for serving

1. To make the salsa: In a medium bowl, combine the pineapple, avocado, bell pepper, onion, jalapeño, cilantro, oil, lime zest and juice, Tajín (if using), and salt and pepper to taste. Taste and adjust the seasoning as needed.

2. To make the crema: In a small bowl, whisk together the yogurt, lime zest and juice, and honey until smooth. Taste and adjust the seasoning as needed.

3. To cook the shrimp: Toss the shrimp with 1 tablespoon of the oil and all the dried seasonings.

4. Preheat a wide, preferably nonstick, skillet over medium heat until hot. Swirl in the remaining 1 tablespoon oil. Add the shrimp and cook until they turn pink all over and are firm, about 1½ minutes per side. Stir in the lime juice and remove from the heat.

5. To assemble: Scoop 3 shrimp onto each lettuce leaf, treating it like a taco shell, and top with spoonfuls of the salsa and crema. Garnish with the sesame seeds, Tajín (if using), and cilantro.

6. Serve hot or warm with the pickled red onions on the side.

ROASTED VEGGIE "PIZZA"

This popular, low-carb recipe seriously scratches the pizza itch, even though it's just a big, healthy serving of vegetables! The method is very clever, turning roasted vegetables into the "crust" of the pizza. I make this whenever my crisper drawers are overloaded with produce, and I need to make some space. And most important, everyone at the dinner table is invariably very happy, too.

Serves 8
Ready in 1 hour

Olive oil cooking spray, for greasing the pan
2 medium zucchini (6 to 8 ounces each), sliced into half-moons
1 pound button mushrooms, cut into large chunks
2 red bell peppers, sliced into strips
3 small crowns broccoli, cut into large florets
Greek olive oil, for drizzling
Fine sea salt and freshly ground black pepper
1 cup grated Parmesan cheese
½ cup fine dried bread crumbs
3 large garlic cloves, minced
2 teaspoons Italian seasoning
1 cup store-bought marinara sauce
10 cherry tomatoes, halved
1 small red onion, sliced
2 cups shredded mozzarella cheese (8 ounces)
Fresh basil leaves, for garnish
Red chile flakes, for garnish

Note: Leftovers heat up amazingly well either on the stovetop in a skillet or in a toaster oven.

1. Preheat the oven to 400°F. Spray a standard 18 by 13-inch baking sheet with the cooking spray.

2. Pile the zucchini, mushrooms, bell peppers, and broccoli on the pan and spread them evenly—it doesn't matter if they are overlapping. Drizzle generously with oil and add salt and pepper to taste.

3. Transfer the pan to the oven and roast for 20 minutes.

4. Meanwhile, in a small bowl, stir together the Parmesan, bread crumbs, garlic, Italian seasoning, and a few pinches of salt and pepper.

5. After the vegetables have roasted for 20 minutes, remove the pan from the oven and gently stir to mix them up. If there is a lot of liquid in the pan, use paper towels to soak most of it up.

6. Nudge the veggies together to form an even rectangle, leaving about an inch between the edges of the pan and the vegetables. Spoon the marinara over the vegetables, then top with the Parmesan mixture. Arrange the tomatoes, onions, and mozzarella on top. Drizzle with more oil.

7. Return the pan to the oven and bake until the cheese is melted and lightly browned, 18 to 20 minutes.

8. Remove the pan from the oven and garnish with the basil and chile flakes.

9. Slice and serve hot.

Change It Up

Easy swaps: Almost any vegetable works in the "crust" using this method—cauliflower, eggplant, butternut squash, Brussels sprouts . . . Get creative!

Make it gluten-free: Swap superfine almond flour for the bread crumbs.

VEGETABLE-STUFFED PORTOBELLOS

Stuffed portobellos are a classic vegetarian main dish, and rather than filling them with rice or another grain, I always opt for colorful vegetables as the primary filling. This ensures that they are, one, full of flavor, and two, low-carb and loaded with nutrients. They don't *need* to be topped with cheese, but you know by now that I rarely pass up such an opportunity. Topping them with slices of something pungent, like Gouda, Gruyère, Taleggio, fontina, or even aged provolone, really makes them special.

Serves 4
Ready in 40 minutes

- 4 large or 8 small portobello mushrooms, stems removed
- 3 tablespoons Greek olive oil, plus more for drizzling
- ½ teaspoon fine sea salt, plus more to taste
- 1 medium zucchini (6 to 8 ounces), diced
- 1 yellow squash (about 5 ounces), diced
- ½ red bell pepper, diced
- 1 medium carrot, diced
- ¾ cup halved cherry tomatoes
- 2 cups baby spinach (2 ounces)
- 2 tablespoons balsamic vinegar
- ¼ cup minced fresh parsley, plus more for garnish
- ¼ cup fine dried bread crumbs
- 1½ cups shredded Gouda, Gruyère, fontina, or Taleggio cheese
- Red chile flakes, for garnish

Change It Up
Make it gluten-free: Substitute superfine almond flour or gluten-free bread crumbs for the bread crumbs.

1. Preheat the oven to 400°F. Line a standard 18 by 13-inch baking sheet with parchment paper.

2. Arrange the mushrooms on the prepared pan and drizzle with a bit of oil, rubbing it all over the caps. Sprinkle lightly with the salt. Turn gill-sides down.

3. Transfer the pan to the oven and bake until juicy and just tender when you insert a paring knife into the center of one, 10 to 15 minutes.

4. Remove the pan from the oven, flip the mushrooms over, and gently blot them with a paper towel to soak up excess moisture and allow to cool slightly. Leave the oven on.

5. Meanwhile, preheat a wide skillet over medium-high heat until hot. Swirl in the oil. Add the zucchini, yellow squash, bell pepper, carrot, and a few pinches of salt, and cook, stirring periodically, until almost tender, 5 to 7 minutes.

6. Add the tomatoes and spinach and stir until the spinach is wilted and the tomatoes have softened slightly, about 2 minutes. Increase the heat and add the vinegar. Continue cooking until the vinegar has mostly cooked off.

7. Remove the pan from the heat and stir in the parsley and bread crumbs. Allow to cool for about 5 minutes.

8. Divide the vegetables among the mushroom caps (don't be afraid to pile them on). Top with the cheese. Return the pan to the oven and bake until the cheese is melted and lightly browned, about 10 minutes more.

9. Remove the pan from the oven and garnish the mushrooms with a bit more parsley and a few pinches of chile flakes.

10. Serve hot.

CREAMY ZUCCHINI & WHITE BEAN SOUP

Beans figure prominently in Greek cuisine, since they are a humble, nourishing ingredient almost everyone can afford. I grew up eating a lot of them in dishes like the classic Greek soup fasolada. This creamy pureed soup is made from equal parts zucchini and white beans. Combining the two has the effect of lessening the carbs somewhat, but more important, the puree transforms two humble ingredients into a silky, luxurious soup that has incredible depth of flavor. You'd never guess it's so quick and easy to make. I love to go crazy with the toppings, which elevate it to fancy fare.

Serves 4 to 6
Ready in 40 minutes

2 tablespoons Greek olive oil, plus more for garnish
1 small sweet onion, diced
3 garlic cloves, minced
4 medium zucchini (6 to 8 ounces each), cut into chunks
1 teaspoon Italian seasoning
4 cups low-sodium chicken or vegetable broth
2 (15-ounce) cans cannellini beans, drained and rinsed
Parmesan rind (optional)
1 teaspoon fine sea salt
Freshly ground black pepper, plus more for garnish
2 cups baby spinach (2 ounces)
Freshly grated Parmesan cheese, for topping
Greek yogurt or sour cream, for topping
Chopped chives, for garnish
Chopped fresh basil or parsley, for garnish
Lemon wedges, for squeezing

1. Preheat a large soup pot over medium heat until hot. Swirl in the oil. Add the onion and sauté until translucent, 3 to 4 minutes. Stir in the garlic, zucchini, and Italian seasoning and sauté until the zucchini begins to soften, 4 to 5 minutes. Add the broth, beans, Parmesan rind (if using), salt, and pepper to taste. Bring to a boil. Turn down the heat to a simmer, cover, and cook until the zucchini is tender, about 10 minutes. Stir in the baby spinach and pick out the Parmesan rind (if using).

2. Use an immersion blender to puree the soup until smooth. (Alternatively, puree in batches in a countertop blender and return it to the soup pot.) Cook over medium heat for another 10 minutes. Taste and adjust the seasoning as needed.

3. Divide the soup among bowls and serve hot, topped liberally with the Parmesan and yogurt. Garnish with a few grinds of pepper, a drizzle of oil, and a sprinkling of chives and basil. Serve with lemon wedges on the side for squeezing.

ROASTED GARLIC GIRL SOUP

In Greece, garlic and olive oil are considered cure-alls, prescribed so widely for various ailments that sometimes it seems it's just a perk that they're such delicious ingredients to cook with! As a card-carrying garlic girl, this blended vegetable soup puts the sweet, intoxicating flavor of roasted garlic front and center, and I tend to make it whenever I'm feeling under the weather, channeling my Greek instincts. I also like to customize it a bit, depending on my mood, adding shredded chicken breast for extra protein or even a few handfuls of greens like spinach or shredded kale for a little nutrient boost.

Serves 4
Ready in 1 hour

1½ pounds Yukon gold potatoes, peeled and cut into ¾-inch chunks
1 large sweet potato, peeled and cut into ¾-inch chunks
1 large carrot, peeled and cut into ¾-inch chunks
1 large red onion, sliced into thick strips
4 garlic heads, tops trimmed away ½ inch to expose the cloves
¼ cup Greek olive oil, plus more for drizzling
Fine sea salt
½ teaspoon red chile flakes, plus more for garnish
Freshly ground black pepper
4 cups low-sodium vegetable or chicken broth
¾ cup heavy cream
¼ cup freshly grated Parmesan cheese
Crispy Shallots (page 212), for garnish

1. Preheat the oven to 400°F. Line a standard 18 by 13-inch sheet pan with parchment paper.

2. Spread the vegetables and garlic heads on the prepared pan and toss with the oil, 1 teaspoon salt, chile flakes, and pepper to taste. Cover the pan tightly with aluminum foil.

3. Transfer the pan to the oven and bake for 20 minutes. Remove the foil and continue cooking until the vegetables are caramelized and tender and the garlic is soft, another 20 to 25 minutes.

4. Remove the pan from the oven and let cool until the garlic is safe to handle, about 15 minutes.

5. Scrape the vegetables (and any juices on the pan) into a soup pot and squeeze the roasted garlic straight into the pot. Cover with the broth and use an immersion blender to puree the soup until smooth. (Alternatively, puree the veggies, broth, and roasted garlic cloves in batches in a countertop blender, then pour into a soup pot.)

6. Return the pot to the heat and bring the soup to a simmer. Cook for 10 minutes, then stir in the cream and Parmesan. Taste and add more salt and pepper if needed.

7. Serve hot, garnished with the crispy shallots, a drizzle of oil, and a pinch of chile flakes.

Change It Up

Make it vegan: Substitute a 15-ounce can of coconut milk for the heavy cream and nutritional yeast for the Parmesan.

Amp it up: Add a scoop of shredded chicken or chickpeas to each serving.

HOW I COOK BACON In a wide, cold skillet, arrange as many slices of bacon as will fit in a single layer. Set the pan over medium-low heat and cook, turning the slices with tongs every few minutes, until evenly browned and crisp, 10 to 15 minutes. Transfer to paper towels to drain and cool.

MICRO CHOP SALAD
with Goddess Dressing

In my family, Thanksgiving wouldn't be complete if I didn't make this micro chop salad. Because holiday fare can be so rich and savory, I find that everyone craves something bright and refreshing to serve as a point of contrast, and this salad always fits the bill. This recipe is especially festive for the occasion because it coincides with when pomegranates are in season (though if you don't have pomegranates, swap in something else that's tart and sweet, like dried cranberries or cherries). Furthermore, lean into its inherent flexibility by incorporating your favorite veggies as you please. But don't mess with the goddess dressing—it is next-level delicious and might be the best part.

Serves 4
Ready in 40 minutes

- 2 heads romaine lettuce, chopped into small pieces
- 2 cups finely shredded red cabbage (about ¼ head)
- 1 large carrot, shredded
- 1 large avocado, diced
- 1 large cucumber, peeled and diced
- 1 cup frozen corn kernels, thawed and blotted dry
- 1 cup pomegranate arils (from 1 pomegranate)
- 8 slices bacon, cooked (see page 184) and chopped or crumbled
- ¼ cup sesame seeds, toasted or raw
- ¼ cup sunflower seeds, roasted or raw
- 1 tablespoon red chile flakes, plus more as needed
- Goddess Dressing (recipe follows)

1. In a large salad bowl, combine all the vegetables, pomegranate arils, bacon, sesame and sunflower seeds, and chile flakes. Taste and add more chile flakes if needed.

2. When ready to serve, add the dressing to taste and toss well.

Change It Up

Amp it up: This is a substantial salad as is, but for an extra protein boost, add 2 crumbled boiled eggs, 1 to 2 cups of leftover shredded chicken, or 2 cans of your favorite beans, drained and rinsed.

Make it vegetarian or vegan: Omit the bacon and use vegan mayonnaise in the dressing.

GODDESS DRESSING
Makes about ¾ cup

- ¼ cup mayonnaise or sour cream
- 3 tablespoons Greek olive oil, plus more as needed
- 1 tablespoon yellow mustard, plus more as needed
- 2 tablespoons maple syrup or honey
- 2 tablespoons fresh lemon juice (1 medium lemon), plus more as needed
- 1 tablespoon apple cider vinegar, plus more as needed
- Fine sea salt and freshly ground black pepper
- 1 tablespoon finely minced fresh chives

In a small bowl, combine all of the ingredients and whisk until smooth and emulsified. Taste and adjust the flavors, adding additional mustard, lemon juice, salt, and pepper as needed. If the dressing is too thick, whisk in an additional tablespoon of oil.

THE ULTIMATE COBB SALAD

This crowd-pleasing, substantial salad may require a bit more prep than most other salads, but it's well worth the extra effort. It's also incredibly flexible and forgiving as a vehicle for odds and ends like leftover rotisserie chicken or another cooked protein, or whatever substitutes you prefer, such as different lettuces, herbs, or cheese. And if you're into meal prepping, mark this page: By cooking the chicken and bacon, boiling the eggs, and making the dressing in advance, all you need to do is to assemble everything together in a salad bowl when it comes time to serve.

Serves 4
Ready in 1 hour

2 teaspoons Greek olive oil
2 boneless, skinless chicken breasts
Fine sea salt
2 large eggs

Dressing
½ cup Greek olive oil
3 tablespoons balsamic vinegar
1 tablespoon honey
1 teaspoon Dijon mustard
1 small garlic clove, minced
1 tablespoon freshly grated Parmesan cheese
¼ teaspoon red chile flakes
¼ teaspoon fine sea salt
Freshly ground black pepper

Salad
2 heads romaine lettuce, chopped
2 plum tomatoes, diced
3 Persian (mini) cucumbers, peeled and sliced
2 small avocados, sliced
¼ red onion, thinly sliced
1 cup frozen sweet corn kernels, thawed and blotted dry
6 slices bacon, cooked (see page 184) and chopped or crumbled
2 ounces blue cheese or Greek feta cheese, crumbled (about ½ cup)
Freshly ground black pepper, for garnish
¼ cup chopped fresh chives, plus more for garnish

1. Rub the oil evenly over the chicken breasts and season with a few pinches of salt on each side.

2. Preheat a nonstick medium skillet over medium heat until hot. Add the chicken breasts and cook until an instant-read thermometer reads 165°F and the meat is fully cooked through, 4 to 6 minutes per side. Rest for 5 minutes, then cut into cubes.

3. Set up a bowl of ice and water. Bring a small saucepan of water to a gentle boil. Gently lower the eggs into the water. Cook for 4 minutes (or up to 7 minutes if you don't like a runny yolk), then transfer the eggs to the ice bath to halt the cooking. Once cool, peel the eggs and quarter or coarsely chop them.

4. To make the dressing: In a screw-top jar or bowl, combine the oil, vinegar, honey, mustard, garlic, Parmesan, chile flakes, salt, and pepper. Shake or whisk until combined. Taste and adjust the seasoning as needed.

5. To assemble the salad: Pile the lettuce into a shallow, wide serving bowl and arrange all the toppings, including the chicken and eggs, on top in colorful strips or piles.

6. Just before serving, drizzle with the dressing and garnish with the pepper and a sprinkling of chives. Toss at the table.

Change It Up

Make it vegetarian or vegan: Substitute 1 can of drained and rinsed chickpeas for the chicken, and either omit the cheese or use your favorite vegan alternative.

ON THE SIDE

Vegetables have always been a huge source of inspiration for me, and I love to turn them into side dishes that present everyday staples in new, unforgettable ways. Some of my most popular recipes, such as Crispy Parmesan Carrot Sticks (page 200) and Cauliflower Steaks Parmesan (page 196), are sides—and I'll never tire of devising new approaches that give this sometimes-neglected part of the meal a little bit of star treatment. Collected here are some of my favorite dishes for holidays, dinner parties, and other celebratory occasions, as well as a few of my go-to salads for rounding out weekday meals.

FRESH ZUCCHINI NOODLE SALAD

Ever since I bought a "zoodler"—a handy tool for quickly turning zucchini into long, curly noodles—I regularly use it to make zucchini noodle salads. In the summer, these noodles are just what I crave, so light and fresh, and there's no pot of boiling water required. This healthy low-carb recipe is chock-full of veggies and highlights many of my favorite nutrient-dense Mediterranean foods, including a mix of olives, toasted nuts, and plenty of fragrant fresh herbs. But because raw zucchini will begin to weep as soon as it comes into contact with anything salty, don't let the tossed salad sit for too long before eating it.

Serves 4
Ready in 25 minutes

- 1 pound spiralized zucchini (zucchini noodles)
- ½ red bell pepper, very thinly sliced
- ¼ medium red onion, very thinly sliced
- 1 teaspoon Italian seasoning
- ½ teaspoon fine sea salt
- ¼ cup Greek olive oil
- 2 tablespoons balsamic vinegar
- 8 Kalamata olives, pitted and halved
- 8 Greek green olives, pitted and halved
- ⅓ cup chopped toasted walnuts, pistachios, or almonds
- ¼ cup chopped fresh mint
- ¼ cup chopped fresh parsley
- Freshly ground black pepper, for garnish

1. In a bowl, toss together the zucchini, bell pepper, onion, Italian seasoning, and salt. Allow to sit for a few minutes while you make the dressing.

2. In a screw-top jar or small bowl, shake or whisk together the oil and vinegar to make a dressing.

3. Add both olives, the nuts, and dressing to the zucchini bowl and toss to combine.

4. Just before serving, sprinkle the mint and parsley over the top and garnish with pepper. Over time, water will be drawn out of the zucchini, so it's best to serve this salad within a half hour or so of making it.

Note: If you don't have a zoodler (or spiralizer), you can make zucchini noodles by hand by slicing the zucchini first into very thin slabs (a mandoline is helpful), stacking a few on top of each other, and then carefully slicing them into long, thin strips using a sturdy, sharp chef's knife.

Change It Up

Amp it up: Top each serving with a few grilled or poached shrimp, ½ to 1 cup drained and rinsed cooked chickpeas, or good-quality canned tuna.

SPICED TAHINI SQUASH
with Lime & Feta

This simple dish of spiced, roasted squash, which is drizzled with tahini and topped with crumbled feta, may not look like much and might even sound like a wildcard mix of flavors. But I consider it a "sleeper side," because it's always the first platter to be wiped clean at the dinner table. When I can restrain myself from eating the whole tray, it is an excellent side at the holidays and works equally well for making ahead, because it tastes just as good at room temperature as it does warm.

Serves 4
Ready in 1 hour

1 large butternut squash (about 3 pounds), peeled and stemmed
3 tablespoons Greek olive oil
1½ teaspoons ground cinnamon
½ teaspoon ground cumin
1 teaspoon fine sea salt
½ cup well-stirred tahini
3 tablespoons fresh lime juice (2 small limes)
1 tablespoon maple syrup or honey
1 ounce Greek feta cheese, crumbled (about ¼ cup)
Coarsely chopped pistachios, everything bagel seasoning, or toasted sesame seeds, for garnish

1. Preheat the oven to 425°F. Line a standard 18 by 13-inch sheet pan with parchment paper.

2. Slice the squash in half through the stem and scoop the seeds out. Slice it crosswise into ¼-inch-thick half-moons. Place the squash in the prepared pan and toss with the oil, cinnamon, cumin, and ½ teaspoon of the salt. Spread out the squash evenly.

3. Transfer the pan to the oven and roast the squash until tender and caramelized at the edges, 35 to 45 minutes, flipping halfway through.

4. Meanwhile, in a small bowl, whisk together the tahini, lime juice, maple syrup, and the remaining ½ teaspoon salt until smooth. Whisk in water 1 tablespoon at a time, until you reach a drippy consistency. Taste and adjust the seasoning as needed.

5. Remove the pan from the oven and spread the squash over a serving platter. Drizzle the sauce all over and top with the feta cheese.

6. Garnish with a sprinkling of pistachios and serve hot, warm, or at room temperature.

Change It Up
Easy swaps: Use sweet potato instead of butternut squash, lemon juice for the lime, or well-stirred peanut butter or almond butter for the tahini.

GREEK LAYERED POTATO BAKE

If you have random cravings for carby potatoes every now and then, like I do, this is the dish to make. With a crunchy, herby bread crumb topping and succulently tender vegetables underneath, it always hits the spot. It's also easy to assemble and feeds a crowd, making it perfect to serve alongside roasts and grilled meats at holidays and dinner parties. The simplicity of it—just layered rounds of potatoes, tomatoes, onion, feta, and a generous drizzle of olive oil—reminds me of the traditional Greek food that my yiayia would cook that always let good ingredients shine.

Serves 8
Ready in 1 hour 15 minutes

Seasoned Bread Crumbs

¾ cup fine dried bread crumbs
⅓ cup grated Parmesan cheese
3 garlic cloves, minced
3 tablespoons Greek olive oil
1 teaspoon Italian seasoning
½ teaspoon red chile flakes

Potato Bake

6 tablespoons Greek olive oil, plus more for brushing
2 pounds Yukon gold potatoes, sliced into ⅛- to ¼-inch-thick rounds
Fine sea salt
2 teaspoons Italian seasoning
1½ pounds plum tomatoes, sliced into rounds
2 medium sweet onions, sliced into rounds
1 (7- to 8-ounce) block Greek feta cheese, crumbled (about 2 cups)

1. Preheat the oven to 375°F.

2. To make the bread crumbs: In a small bowl, stir together all the ingredients.

3. To assemble the potato bake: Drizzle the bottom of a 9 by 13-inch baking dish or pan with 2 tablespoons of the oil and arrange half of the potato slices in a shingled pattern. Lightly brush the tops with some oil, season with a few pinches of salt, and 1 teaspoon of the Italian seasoning. Arrange half the tomatoes and onions on top. Crumble the feta on top and drizzle with another 2 tablespoons oil. Repeat the layering with the remaining potatoes, Italian seasoning, onions, tomatoes, and the remaining 2 tablespoons oil. Sprinkle the bread crumb mixture evenly over the bake.

4. Transfer the pan to the oven and bake until the potatoes are fork-tender, 1 hour to 1 hour 15 minutes. For darker browning on the topping, switch the oven to broil and place the pan beneath the heat source for 1 to 3 minutes, watching carefully.

5. Remove the pan from the oven and serve hot or warm.

CAULIFLOWER STEAKS PARMESAN

Think of these cheese-topped cauliflower steaks as the vegetarian answer to chicken parm, a classic Italian-American dish in the northeastern United States and one of the most popular platters at my dad's diners. In this vegetable-based spin, cauliflower is roasted until caramelized and tender, then dressed up with marinara sauce and melty mozzarella cheese. It makes for a brilliant low-carb side dish, but you could also serve it as a substantial vegetarian main, alongside a simple salad such as Yiayia's Maroulosalata (page 216). This dish is also just as good without the cheese.

Serves 4
Ready in 30 minutes

⅓ cup panko bread crumbs
¼ cup grated Parmesan cheese
½ teaspoon onion powder
½ teaspoon garlic powder
½ teaspoon paprika
½ teaspoon fine sea salt
Freshly ground black pepper
1 large head cauliflower
¼ cup Greek olive oil
⅓ cup store-bought marinara sauce
½ cup coarsely shredded mozzarella cheese
Chopped fresh parsley, for garnish
Chile flakes, for garnish

1. Preheat the oven to 400°F. Line a standard 18 by 13-inch baking sheet with parchment paper.

2. In a wide, shallow dish, mix together the panko, Parmesan, onion powder, garlic powder, paprika, salt, and pepper to taste.

3. Carefully trim away any leaves from the bottom of the cauliflower, taking care to keep the stem whole. Carefully cut the cauliflower in half through the stem, then make a parallel cut through each half, creating four thick slabs. The goal is to keep them all attached by some of the cauliflower stem, but oftentimes the outer cuts will break into a few pieces, which is fine.

4. Generously brush the cauliflower steaks all over with the oil. Then dredge them in the panko mixture to coat. Arrange them in a single layer on the prepared pan.

5. Transfer the pan to the oven and bake until the stems are fork-tender and golden brown, about 25 minutes, carefully flipping them halfway through.

6. Divide the marinara sauce followed by the mozzarella on top of the steaks. Return the pan to the oven and bake until the cheese is melted and lightly blistered, 3 to 5 minutes more.

7. Remove the pan from the oven, garnish with the parsley and chile flakes, and serve hot.

Change It Up

Air-Fried Cauliflower Steaks: Cook the cauliflower steaks in an air-fryer basket at 375°F for 15 to 20 minutes, flipping once. Depending on the size of your fryer, you may need to cook them in two batches.

Amp it up: Top the cauliflower steaks with a grilled or roasted chicken breast, a big spoonful of chickpeas, or your favorite leafy green salad.

ROASTED PESTO CABBAGE WEDGES

An underrated gem, cabbage is inexpensive, nutrient rich, stays fresh for weeks in the refrigerator, and is even a bit of a chameleon in terms of how it can take on so many flavors, depending on how you cook it. This is a simple but spectacular way to showcase the humble cabbage by slathering wedges in homemade pesto and then roasting them in a hot oven. It becomes tender, caramelized, and saturated with all that summery flavor.

Serves 8
Ready in 35 minutes

1 medium head green cabbage
¾ cup basil pesto, homemade (recipe follows) or store-bought
Freshly grated Parmesan cheese, for serving
Chopped fresh parsley, for garnish
Freshly ground black pepper, for garnish
Lemon wedges, for squeezing

Change It Up

Make it spicy: Instead of pesto, whisk ½ cup harissa paste (or less if you prefer less heat) into ¼ cup Greek olive oil, along with a few pinches of salt and pepper, and use this as the marinade for the cabbage.

Easy swaps: Use red, napa, or any other type of cabbage you like.

Make it vegan: Substitute nutritional yeast for the Parmesan or omit the cheese altogether.

1. Preheat the oven to 400°F. Line a standard 18 by 13-inch baking sheet with parchment paper.

2. Slice the cabbage into quarters through the stem, then cut each quarter in half to make eight wedges, all still attached to the stem. Arrange the cabbage on the prepared pan. Divide the pesto evenly all over each cabbage wedge and arrange them cut-side down in the pan.

3. Transfer the pan to the oven and roast the cabbage for 20 minutes. Flip the wedges, then continue roasting until golden brown all over and caramelized at the edges, another 10 to 15 minutes. To achieve darker browning, switch the oven to broil and place the pan beneath the heat source for 1 to 3 minutes, watching carefully.

4. Remove the pan from the oven and serve the cabbage hot or warm, sprinkled with the Parmesan and garnished with the parsley and pepper, with lemon wedges on the side for squeezing.

BASIL PESTO
Makes ¾ cup

4 ounces fresh basil leaves (about 5 ½ cups, gently packed)
2 garlic cloves, peeled
1 tablespoon pine nuts or walnuts
¼ teaspoon fine sea salt
½ cup Greek olive oil
½ cup freshly grated Parmesan cheese

1. Place the blade of a food processor in the refrigerator to chill for 10 to 15 minutes (this helps prevent the basil from oxidizing).

2. Meanwhile, soak the basil in ice water for 10 to 15 minutes, then drain and dry thoroughly in a salad spinner.

3. In the food processor, combine the basil, garlic, and pine nuts and make 1-second pulses until the basil is finely chopped; this will take about 30 seconds. Add the salt. With the motor running, drizzle in the oil. Add the Parmesan and process until the pesto is smooth, about 30 seconds more.

ON THE SIDE

CRISPY PARMESAN CARROT STICKS
with Lazy Tzatziki

This dish essentially combines spiced and caramelized roasted carrots with a crispy cheese chip—two things that are great on their own but even better together. The key is to create a broad, flat side on each carrot piece; that is where you'll adhere the grated cheese before baking everything in the oven. As the carrots cool, the cheese layer gets crispy, creating a delicious contrast of textures. To give the carrots a little Greek flair, I always pair them with my lazy tzatziki for dipping.

Serves 4
Ready in 30 minutes

- 1 pound carrots (4 medium-to-large carrots), peeled if desired
- 2 tablespoons Greek olive oil
- 4 garlic cloves, minced
- 1 cup freshly grated Parmesan cheese
- Heaping ½ teaspoon paprika
- Heaping ½ teaspoon chili powder
- Heaping ½ teaspoon onion powder
- Heaping ½ teaspoon Italian seasoning
- Fine sea salt
- Lazy Tzatziki (recipe follows), for serving

1. Preheat the oven to 425°F.

2. Slice the carrots into 3-inch-long segments, then slice each one in half lengthwise. Each piece should have a flat side.

3. In a small bowl, whisk together the oil, garlic, ¼ cup of the Parmesan, the paprika, chili powder, onion powder, Italian seasoning, and salt to taste. Add the carrots and toss them to evenly coat.

4. Place the remaining ¾ cup Parmesan in a shallow bowl or plate. Working one at a time, dip the flat side of each carrot into the cheese, then place on an unlined standard 18 by 13-inch baking sheet, cheese-side down. (If you're having trouble getting the cheese to stick, just make a little pile of cheese on the baking sheet that matches the size of your carrot and press the carrot onto it.) Space the carrots evenly in the pan.

5. Transfer the pan to the oven and roast until the carrots are tender and the cheese is browned and crisp, 20 to 30 minutes, depending on the thickness of the carrots.

6. Remove the pan from the oven and serve hot or warm, with the lazy tzatziki on the side for dipping.

LAZY TZATZIKI

Tzatziki traditionally includes cucumber, of course, but this is a more pantry-friendly variation that doesn't involve any vegetable prep.

Makes about 1 cup

- 1 cup whole milk Greek yogurt
- 1 tablespoon fresh lemon juice or red wine vinegar
- 1 tablespoon Greek olive oil
- Heaping ½ teaspoon garlic powder
- 1 teaspoon dried mint
- Fine sea salt
- 1 teaspoon sriracha sauce (optional)
- Whole milk, for thinning

In a small bowl, whisk together all the ingredients, adding milk if needed to thin the dip to your liking. Taste and adjust the seasoning as needed. Allow the tzatziki to sit for at least 30 minutes to develop the best flavor.

MEDITERRANEAN VEGGIE STIR-FRY

Packed with the Mediterranean flavors of olives, feta, and parsley, this stir-fry is a superfast way to whip up an ample serving of vegetables that everybody will love. I can happily enjoy a whole pan as a late-night snack, but as a side dish it pairs perfectly with pasta dishes or your favorite grilled meats and seafood, such as steak, chicken, or shrimp. Just be careful not to overcook the vegetables. They're best when crisp-tender, meaning they should still have the faintest bit of crunch and hold their shape after cooking.

Serves 4
Ready in 15 minutes

- 2 tablespoons Greek olive oil, plus more for drizzling
- 1 large red bell pepper, thinly sliced
- 1 pound small broccoli florets (about 5 cups)
- ½ teaspoon fine sea salt
- Freshly ground black pepper
- ⅓ cup low-sodium vegetable or chicken broth
- ⅓ cup Kalamata olives, pitted and halved
- 3 ounces Greek feta cheese, crumbled (about ¾ cup)
- Toasted sesame seeds, for garnish
- Lemon wedges, for squeezing
- Chopped fresh parsley, for garnish

1. Preheat a wide sauté pan or braiser (one that includes a lid) over high heat until hot. Swirl in the oil. Add the bell pepper and broccoli, arranging it in an even layer, then allow it to sear without stirring, about 1 minute. Season with the salt and the pepper to taste, then flip the veggies over. Add the broth, cover the pan, and turn down the heat to medium. Cook until the vegetables are just crisp-tender, 2 to 3 minutes.

2. Add the olives and feta to the pan, cover it again, and cook just until the cheese is softened and heated through, 1 minute more.

3. Serve immediately, garnished with the sesame seeds, spritzes of lemon juice, parsley, and a light drizzle of oil.

Note: If you don't have broth, replace it with ⅓ cup water, ½ teaspoon garlic powder, and ½ teaspoon onion powder whisked together.

Change It Up

Easy swaps: Substitute freshly grated Parmesan for the feta (or omit it altogether to make a dairy-free dish). Zucchini coins, sliced mushrooms, green beans, and cauliflower all work well in this recipe.

ON THE SIDE

SPICED ROASTED ASPARAGUS
over Burrata

Dinner parties are one of the best times to bring out a showstopping side dish, and this one is both quick to make and absolutely unforgettable. It's great served as a first course and plated individually, so each guest can appreciate the stunning combination of colors, flavors, and warm and cool textures, and it looks elegant on a family-style platter, too. The creamy Burrata is such a decadent addition to the sesame seed–roasted asparagus and lightly sweet vinaigrette. Simply put, this is not your average asparagus dish. Round out the menu with grilled chicken, fish, or steak as the entrée.

Serves 4
Ready in 20 minutes

1 pound asparagus, trimmed
2 tablespoons Greek olive oil
4 garlic cloves, minced
2 tablespoons sesame seeds
½ teaspoon paprika
½ teaspoon onion powder
½ teaspoon red chile flakes
½ teaspoon fine sea salt
Freshly ground black pepper

Vinaigrette
3 tablespoons Greek olive oil
2 teaspoons honey
Juice of 1 medium lemon (see Note)
A few pinches of fine sea salt
8 ounces Burrata cheese (four 2-ounce balls)
2 tablespoons chopped fresh dill, for garnish
Grated lemon zest, for garnish

1. Preheat the oven to 425°F. Line a standard 18 by 13-inch baking sheet with parchment paper.

2. In a bowl, toss the asparagus with the oil. Add the garlic, sesame seeds, paprika, onion powder, chile flakes, salt, and pepper to taste. Use your hands to mix so the asparagus is evenly coated in the spice mixture. Space out the asparagus in a single layer on the prepared pan.

3. Transfer the pan to the oven and roast until the asparagus is just fork-tender, 10 to 12 minutes.

4. Meanwhile, to make the dressing: In a small bowl, whisk together all the ingredients.

5. To assemble: Break open the Burrata balls and arrange them on salad plates or a serving platter, then divide the roasted asparagus on top of them. Drizzle the dressing all over.

6. Serve hot or warm, garnished with the dill and lemon zest.

Note: Grate the zest from the lemon before juicing and reserve the zest for garnish.

HONEY-BALSAMIC ROASTED BEETS

Like cabbage, beets are a massively underrated vegetable. They're inexpensive, full of vitamins and nutrients, delicious whether hot or cold, and so easy to prepare—I ate them often growing up. Here, they're roasted in a mixture of balsamic vinegar and honey, which reduces to a sticky glaze that coats each tender bite. Because beets are so welcoming of contrasting textures and flavors, I sometimes add crumbled feta and pickled onions before serving or take things a step further by spooning them over tender salad greens.

Serves 4
Ready in 45 minutes

2 medium red beets (about 8 ounces), peeled and cut into 1-inch chunks
2 medium golden beets (about 8 ounces), peeled and cut into 1-inch chunks
2 large carrots (about 8 ounces), peeled and cut into 1-inch chunks
2 tablespoons Greek olive oil
1 teaspoon dried thyme
1 teaspoon fine sea salt
Freshly ground black pepper
3 tablespoons balsamic vinegar
2 tablespoons honey
Fresh thyme leaves, for garnish

1. Preheat the oven to 425°F. Line a standard 18 by 13-inch baking sheet with parchment paper.

2. Pile the vegetables on the prepared pan and toss with the oil, dried thyme, salt, and pepper to taste until evenly coated. Spread out the vegetables in an even layer.

3. Transfer the pan to the oven and roast for 20 minutes.

4. Meanwhile, in a small bowl, whisk together the balsamic vinegar and honey.

5. Remove the pan from the oven and pour the balsamic mixture over the parcooked vegetables, stirring gently to coat. Return the pan to the oven and roast until the beets are fork-tender and the sauce has thickened slightly, another 10 to 15 minutes.

6. Remove the pan from the oven and serve hot or warm, garnished with the fresh thyme.

HORIATIKI
Classic Greek Salad over White Bean–Feta Whip

Horiatiki is what most Americans think of as Greek salad, with its chunks of tomatoes, cucumbers, feta, and Kalamata olives. For me, it is an everyday salad that I serve regularly. Here, we amp it up a little with added protein and creaminess in the form of a white bean and feta whip. You smear some of the whip over a serving plate and spoon the salad on top so all the fresh, salty juices mingle to create an explosion of flavor—it's a perfect dip to mop up with crusty bread! Use any leftover whip as a dip or spread for sandwiches.

Serves 4 to 6
Ready in 20 minutes

3 plum tomatoes, cut into small chunks
1 large cucumber, peeled and sliced into half-moons
½ small red onion, thinly sliced
1 small green bell pepper, thinly sliced
⅓ cup pitted Kalamata olives
3 tablespoons Greek olive oil
1 tablespoon red wine vinegar
1 teaspoon dried oregano
Fine sea salt
About 2 cups White Bean–Feta Whip (recipe follows), for serving
Lemon zest, for garnish
Dried oregano, for garnish
Freshly ground black pepper, for garnish

1. In a large salad bowl, mix together the tomatoes, cucumber, onion, bell pepper, olives, oil, vinegar, oregano, and a few pinches of salt to taste, tossing to combine.

2. Spread about ⅓ cup of the white bean–feta whip onto each serving plate, smearing it out into an even round. Top with a generous scoop of the salad in the center, garnish with the lemon zest, oregano, and black pepper, and serve right away.

WHITE BEAN–FETA WHIP
Makes about 3 cups

1 (7- to 8-ounce) block Greek feta cheese
1 (15-ounce) can white beans, drained, rinsed, and patted dry
3 tablespoons Greek olive oil
1 garlic clove, peeled but whole
⅓ cup whole milk Greek yogurt
1 teaspoon finely grated lemon zest
1 tablespoon fresh lemon juice (½ medium lemon), plus more as needed
2 teaspoons honey, plus more as needed (optional)
1 to 2 teaspoons ice water

In a food processor, combine all the ingredients (except the water) and pulse until mostly smooth. With the motor running, drizzle in the water a teaspoon at a time, until the mixture becomes just a little bit lighter and is evenly smooth. Avoid adding too much water; that may make the spread too loose. Taste, adding more lemon juice or honey as needed.

Change It Up

Avocado-Feta Spread: Substitute 1 ripe avocado for the yogurt in the spread.

SUMMERY PITA SALAD
with Figs, Peaches, Tomatoes & Corn

When I visit Greece in the summer, I can make a meal out of ripe seasonal fruit, eating fresh figs or a juicy peach out of hand while sitting in the sunshine on the beach. It's heaven! And whenever the produce is so ripe and flavorful, I use a light hand when I cook with it. Tomatoes, raw corn kernels, and sweet, juicy fruit are front and center, and toasted pitas give it a fattoush vibe but more important, they soak up every drop of delicious flavor. It's full-on Greek summer in a bite.

Serves 4 to 6
Ready in 30 minutes

3 pitas, cut or torn into bite-size pieces
2 tablespoons Greek olive oil
Fine sea salt

Dressing
¼ cup Greek olive oil
2 tablespoons fresh lemon juice (1 medium lemon)
2 tablespoons white balsamic vinegar
2 teaspoons honey
1 teaspoon Dijon mustard
¼ teaspoon fine sea salt

Salad
1 peach, pitted and sliced
1 large or 2 medium heirloom tomatoes, cut into large chunks
4 fresh figs, quartered
Kernels from 1 ear corn
2 Persian (mini) cucumbers, sliced
4 ounces Greek feta or Cotija cheese, crumbled (about 1 cup)
1 cup fresh basil or cilantro leaves, torn if large, plus more for garnish

1. Preheat the oven to 425°F. Line a standard 18 by 13-inch baking sheet with parchment paper.

2. Spread out the pita pieces on the prepared pan, drizzle with the oil, and toss to evenly coat.

3. Transfer the pan to the oven and bake until the pitas are lightly browned and mostly crispy (they don't have to be entirely crisp), 12 to 15 minutes, stirring halfway through. Sprinkle lightly with salt, then set aside to cool slightly as you prepare the rest of the salad.

4. To make the dressing: In a salad bowl, whisk together all the ingredients until combined.

5. To assemble the salad: Add the pitas, peach, tomatoes, figs, corn, and cucumbers to the dressing, gently tossing the salad until combined. Let stand for 10 to 15 minutes.

6. Just before serving, stir in the cheese and basil and gently toss to combine. Garnish with additional basil.

FALL BRUSSELS SPROUTS SALAD
with Halloumi, Dates & Crispy Shallots

Brussels sprouts are low in carbs, high in fiber and nutrients, and their flavor can hold up well to assertive dressings and accompaniments, as in this flavor-packed salad. Shaved sprouts are roasted until slightly charred and caramelized; this deepens their flavor and speeds up the typical roasting time. Then things are nudged in a sweet-salty direction by combining the sprouts with crumbled bacon, slivered dates, and pan-seared cubes of salty Halloumi cheese.

Serves 4 to 6
Ready in 45 minutes

1½ pounds Brussels sprouts, ends trimmed
2 tablespoons plus 1 teaspoon Greek olive oil
1 tablespoon maple syrup or honey
¼ teaspoon fine sea salt
4 ounces Halloumi, cut into ½-inch cubes (about 1 cup)

Dressing

¼ cup Greek olive oil
3 tablespoons fresh lemon juice (1½ medium lemons)
1 teaspoon Dijon mustard
1 teaspoon dried oregano
½ teaspoon red chile flakes
Pinch of fine sea salt

Salad

4 slices bacon, cooked (see page 184) and chopped or crumbled
5 Medjool dates, pitted and chopped
¼ cup Favorite Pickled Red Onions (page 119), drained
¼ cup sliced or slivered almonds, toasted
½ cup Crispy Shallots (recipe follows), for garnish
Freshly ground black pepper, for garnish

1. Preheat the oven to 425°F. Line a standard 18 by 13-inch baking sheet with parchment paper.

2. Slice each Brussels sprout in half through the stem. Then, with the flat sides down on the cutting board, make shavings by slicing each one crosswise into thin half-moons. (Alternatively, you can shave them by sending the whole Brussels sprout through the slicing blade of a food processor.) In a bowl, toss them with 2 tablespoons oil, the maple syrup, and salt. Spread out on the prepared pan in an even layer.

3. Transfer the pan to the oven and roast the sprouts until they're tender and caramelized, 18 to 22 minutes.

4. Remove the pan from the oven and set aside to cool.

5. Preheat a nonstick skillet over medium heat until hot. Swirl in the remaining 1 teaspoon oil. Add the Halloumi cubes and sauté, turning them periodically, until golden brown on their tops and bottoms, 1 to 2 minutes per side.

6. Meanwhile, to make the dressing: In a screw-top jar or small bowl, combine all the ingredients and shake or whisk until combined.

7. To assemble the salad: In a large bowl, toss together the roasted Brussels sprouts, most of the warm Halloumi, the bacon, dates, pickled onions, and almonds. Drizzle with the dressing to taste.

8. Serve, garnished with the reserved Halloumi, the crispy shallots, and pepper.

CRISPY SHALLOTS
Makes about 1 cup

2 large shallots, peeled
¼ cup all-purpose flour
Fine sea salt and freshly ground black pepper
2 tablespoons Greek olive oil

1. Using a mandoline or sharp knife, slice the shallots into thin rings. In a small bowl, toss them with the flour and a few pinches of salt and pepper to taste.

2. Preheat a large skillet over medium-high heat until hot. Swirl in the oil. Add the shallots and cook, stirring often, until golden and crispy, 6 to 7 minutes.

Change It Up

Easy swaps: Instead of the dates, use other dried fruit, such as cranberries, raisins, or dried cherries, or fresh pomegranate arils. You'll need about ⅓ cup.

CAULIFLOWER WEDGE SALAD
with Bacon & Blue Cheese Dressing

If you're enthusiastic about a good steak house–style wedge salad with crispy bacon crumbles, ripe tomatoes, and creamy blue cheese dressing, then you'll love this wedge salad variation. Cauliflower is quartered and brushed with a cheesy, herby, flavor-packed oil and then lightly charred and caramelized in the hot oven. To serve, it gets the classic wedge treatment, featuring my favorite (and easiest) blue cheese dressing.

Serves 4
Ready in 35 minutes

Roasted Cauliflower
Olive oil cooking spray, for spraying the parchment
1 large head cauliflower
¼ cup Greek olive oil
2 tablespoons grated Parmesan cheese
½ teaspoon garlic powder
½ teaspoon onion powder
½ teaspoon paprika
Fine sea salt and freshly ground black pepper

Dressing
2½ ounces crumbled blue cheese (heaping ½ cup)
¼ cup whole milk Greek yogurt or sour cream
2 tablespoons buttermilk or kefir
1 garlic clove, minced
2 tablespoons minced fresh chives
Fine sea salt and freshly ground black pepper

Assembly
2½ ounces crumbled blue cheese (heaping ½ cup)
4 slices bacon, cooked (see page 184) and chopped or crumbled
1 cup cherry tomatoes, halved
Freshly ground black pepper, for garnish
Chopped fresh chives, for garnish

1. To roast the cauliflower: Preheat the oven to 450°F. Line a standard 18 by 13-inch sheet pan with parchment paper and lightly spray it with the cooking spray.

2. Trim off the leaves and bottom part of the stem from the cauliflower. Slice it into quarters through the stem and arrange the pieces cut-side down in the prepared pan.

3. In a small bowl, stir together the oil, Parmesan, garlic powder, onion powder, paprika, and a few pinches of salt and pepper. Brush this mixture all over the cauliflower pieces. Cover the pan with aluminum foil.

4. Transfer the pan to the oven and bake until the cauliflower is tender, about 25 minutes.

5. Meanwhile, to make the dressing: In a small bowl, combine the blue cheese with the rest of the dressing ingredients in a small bowl. Taste and adjust the seasoning as needed.

6. Once the cauliflower is tender, remove the foil, switch the oven to broil, place the pan under the heat source, and broil for 1 to 3 minutes, watching carefully, until the cauliflower pieces are nicely browned.

7. To assemble: Remove the pan from the oven and transfer the cauliflower to a serving platter (or serve directly from the sheet pan if you like!). Spoon the dressing over the cauliflower wedges. Top with the blue cheese, bacon, and tomatoes.

8. Serve warm or at room temperature, garnished with the pepper and chives.

Change It Up

Easy swaps: Use this treatment for roasted cabbage or broccoli wedges.

YIAYIA'S MAROULOSALATA
Romaine Salad with Scallions & Dill

FAN FAVORITE

While horiatiki (see page 208) is probably the most well-known Greek salad in the United States, maroulosalata is arguably more of a classic in Greek homes. Brightly flavored with plenty of lemon juice, scallions, and fresh dill, it was the go-to salad my yiayia and mom made while I was growing up, and while it took me a while to appreciate the flavor of dill, this salad eventually became one of my favorites, too. Traditionally, maroulosalata doesn't include feta, but my family always added it, so it feels traditional to me. Two important notes: Be sure to slice the romaine thinly, because you don't want big pieces of lettuce. Second, toss the salad by hand so the dressing is well distributed and the cheese is incorporated into every bite—I find it to be a therapeutic process.

Serves 4
Ready in 15 minutes

- 2 hearts romaine lettuce, separated into leaves
- ½ cup Greek olive oil
- ¼ cup fresh lemon juice (2 medium lemons)
- ¼ teaspoon fine sea salt
- 1 bunch of scallions (4 or 5), green and white parts, thinly sliced
- 1 bunch of fresh dill, finely chopped
- 4 ounces Greek feta cheese, crumbled (about 1 cup)

1. If the lettuce is wet at all, run it through your salad spinner a few times to ensure it's thoroughly dry. Using a sharp knife, cut the romaine into very thin strips by stacking a few leaves on top of each other and slicing them into thin ribbons.

2. In a small bowl, whisk together the oil, lemon juice, and salt until smooth and thick.

3. Place the lettuce, scallions, dill, and feta in a large bowl and drizzle with the dressing. Use your hands to toss the salad, gently massaging and scrunching the greens so they soften slightly and are well coated in cheese and dressing.

Change It Up

Amp it up: Top each serving with a sliced chicken breast, ½ to 1 cup drained and rinsed cooked chickpeas, or your favorite protein to turn it into a meal.

Make it vegan: Substitute 1 ripe avocado, cut into cubes, for the feta cheese.

SWEET SPOT

In Greek culture, dessert is typically reserved for special occasions rather than an everyday thing. I was taught to reach for fresh fruit or a Medjool date to satisfy my sweet tooth, and I still try to make this my default. But if you've been following me for a while, you know that I also love a healthy homemade dessert that uses good fats, natural sweeteners instead of granulated sugar, and has fewer carbs—so I can feel good about sharing these treats with my kids and indulging in them every now and then. You'll find many of those types of recipes in this chapter, as well as some of the traditional Greek desserts that my family makes for birthdays, holidays, and anytime there's something special to celebrate.

NO-BAKE STRAWBERRY TIRAMISU

Tiramisu can come in different flavors besides the classic espresso one, and this is a stunning variation. It's the perfect dessert to capitalize on strawberry season, because it gets shingled with sliced berries in a gorgeous flower pattern, always eliciting lots of *oohs* and *aahs* at the table. Yes, there are three bowls involved, and there's a bit of an assembly required, but I promise you that the finished result is entirely worth the effort. If you don't want to open a full-size bottle of prosecco, a small amount of which is used in the mixture that the ladyfingers are dipped in, a single-serving–size bottle comes in handy.

Serves 9
Ready in 18 hours

1 pound strawberries
2 tablespoons granulated sugar
Grated zest of 1 orange
Pinch of fine sea salt
¾ cup heavy cream
1 cup mascarpone
½ cup confectioners' sugar
½ teaspoon vanilla extract
⅔ cup strawberry preserves
½ cup prosecco
1 teaspoon balsamic vinegar or lemon juice
1 (7-ounce) package ladyfingers

1. Set aside about half the strawberries to use as garnish for serving. Hull and slice the remaining strawberries and add to a bowl. Add the granulated sugar, orange zest, and salt and stir to combine. Allow to macerate for 10 to 15 minutes.

2. Meanwhile, in a separate bowl, using a handheld electric mixer, whip the cream until soft peaks form. Blend in the mascarpone, confectioners' sugar, and vanilla just until the mixture is smooth.

3. In a shallow bowl, stir together the strawberry preserves, prosecco, and vinegar.

4. Working a few at a time, dip half the ladyfingers into the liquid, turning them so they're well coated all over. Arrange them in an even, single layer in an 8 by 8-inch baking dish, breaking them into smaller pieces if necessary to fill the entire surface area. Spread half the cream-mascarpone mixture evenly over the ladyfingers, then layer the macerated strawberries over the cream. Repeat this process with another layer of dipped ladyfingers and the remaining cream. Cover the dish tightly with plastic wrap and refrigerate overnight.

5. When ready to serve, hull the remaining strawberries and slice them through the stem. Arrange them in a flower pattern on top of the tiramisu by spiraling them from the outside of the pan toward the center, with the tips of the strawberries pointing out like petals.

6. Slice into nine squares, wiping the knife clean between cuts for neat pieces. Use a thin spatula to scoop pieces out of the pan. Store leftovers covered with plastic wrap in the refrigerator for up to 2 days.

Change It Up

For a nonalcoholic version: Substitute freshly squeezed orange juice for the prosecco.

Swap the fruit: Use sliced peaches or nectarines, raspberries, or blackberries.

MAMA'S JUICY FRUIT SALAD

Every Drivas family function requires an enormous bowl of my mom's beloved fruit salad, featuring a variety of fruits that changes with the seasons. When my brother and I were kids, fruit was the only option for satisfying our sweet cravings after dinner, so it seems perfectly natural to have this recipe in this chapter. But even when there are pies, cakes, and other more traditional sweet treats, Mom still adds this salad to the menu. It's always so appreciated as a fresh, healthy option after a big, rich meal. The lime and mint dressing might seem unusual, but it is key to the recipe, leveling it up from a standard-fare fruit platter.

Serves 10
Ready in 30 minutes

Dressing
- 2 tablespoons maple syrup or honey
- Grated zest of 1 lime
- Juice of 2 large limes
- 8 fresh mint leaves, sliced into thin strips

Salad
- 1 pound strawberries, hulled and halved
- 1 pint blueberries
- 3 kiwi, peeled and cut into bite-size chunks
- 3 champagne mangoes, peeled and cut into bite-size chunks
- 1 pint blackberries
- 1 pint raspberries
- ½ honeydew melon, peeled, seeded, and cut into bite-size chunks

1. To make the dressing: In a bowl, whisk together all the dressing ingredients and allow to sit for at least 30 minutes for the flavors to combine.

2. To assemble the salad: In a large salad bowl, toss the fruits together with the dressing until well coated. It can sit for a few hours but should be eaten on the day that it's made.

Change It Up

Easy swaps: Any of the following fruits work well in this salad: halved grapes, small pineapple chunks, pitted and halved cherries, watermelon chunks, cubed peaches, cubed nectarines—or whatever fruit catches your eye at a farmers' market or grocery store.

LIGHTER BAKLAVA CHEESECAKE BARS

Cheesecake has become something of a family affair for me. In my dad's early work in the United States as a baker, everyone loved his desserts. But it was his cheesecake, piled high with glazed strawberries and whipped cream, that was absolutely his specialty. Since I'm always looking for ways to make my favorite treats a little healthier, I've incorporated cottage cheese into the filling for these cheesecake bars; that lightens things up and improves its protein, too. And rather than strawberries, I've topped them with the sweet, nutrient-rich nutty filling typically used in baklava. My dad would be so proud of this dessert!

Makes 16 small squares or 9 larger squares
Ready in 2½ hours

Phyllo Crust
4 tablespoons unsalted butter, melted
6 (14 by 18-inch, #4) frozen phyllo sheets, thawed overnight in the refrigerator

Filling
1 (8-ounce) package cream cheese, at room temperature
1 (16-ounce) container whole milk cottage cheese
½ cup granulated sugar
⅓ cup sour cream or whole-milk Greek yogurt
3 large eggs, at room temperature
2 teaspoons vanilla extract
5 tablespoons tapioca flour or cornstarch

Topping
½ cup honey
½ cup water
1 small cinnamon stick
½ cup chopped walnuts
¼ cup chopped pistachios or almonds
1 tablespoon grated lemon zest

1. To make the crust: Preheat the oven to 425°F. Line an 8 by 8-inch baking pan with parchment paper (see my parchment-lining tip on page 40), leaving overhang on the sides so the cake can be lifted out later. Brush the bottom with some of the melted butter.

2. Cut the phyllo sheets in half, so they're roughly the width of the baking pan. Working quickly to prevent the phyllo from drying out, layer the phyllo into the pan, brushing each sheet evenly with the melted butter.

3. Transfer the pan to the oven and bake the phyllo until lightly browned, about 5 minutes.

4. Remove the pan from the oven and set aside to cool on a wire rack, while you prepare the filling. Lower the oven temperature to 325°F.

5. To make the filling: In a food processor, combine the cream cheese, cottage cheese, sugar, and sour cream and process until smooth and light. Add the eggs and vanilla and process until evenly combined, scraping the sides and bottom once or twice as needed. Finally, pulse in the tapioca flour. Pour the batter into the crust and tap it on the countertop a few times to eliminate any air bubbles.

6. Return the pan to the oven and bake the cheesecake until just set (a little bit of jiggle is fine), 40 to 45 minutes.

7. Remove the pan from the oven and cool on a wire rack for 30 minutes, then transfer the pan to the refrigerator to cool the cheesecake completely until firm and set, at least 1 hour.

8. To make the topping: In a small saucepan, combine the honey, water, and the cinnamon stick and bring to a boil over medium-high heat. Immediately turn down the heat and simmer until the mixture thickens slightly, about 10 minutes, stirring occasionally (it will thicken further as it cools).

9. Remove the pot from the heat and pick out the cinnamon stick. Stir in the nuts and lemon zest. Cool completely, at least 1 hour, then pour evenly onto the cooled cheesecake.

10. Use the overhanging parchment to lift the cake from the pan and slice into squares. Packed in an airtight container, leftovers will keep for up to 3 days in the refrigerator or for up to 1 month in the freezer.

VEGAN TAHINI-CHOCOLATE CHUNK COOKIES

These cookies will make tahini lovers happy, because in one sense they're all about that rich and distinctive sesame flavor. However, my kids aren't the biggest fans of tahini, yet they ask for these cookies *all* the time. So, they're equally an all-purpose, one-bowl, vegan chocolate chip cookie that's quick to make from everyday ingredients. And with crispy edges and chewy centers, it's pretty hard to find any fault with them. The sprinkling of flaky salt takes them over the top.

Makes 20 cookies
Ready in 25 minutes

- 1 cup well-stirred tahini, at room temperature
- ¾ cup maple syrup
- ⅓ cup Greek olive oil
- 2 teaspoons vanilla extract
- ½ cup all-purpose flour
- ½ cup superfine almond flour
- ¼ cup tapioca flour
- ¾ teaspoon baking soda
- ¼ teaspoon fine sea salt
- 1 (6-ounce) semisweet chocolate bar, chopped, or 1 cup chips, plus more for topping
- Flaky salt, for garnish

1. Preheat the oven to 350°F. Line two standard 18 by 13-inch baking sheets with parchment paper.

2. In a bowl, whisk together the tahini, maple syrup, oil, and vanilla until smooth. Sift in the three flours, the baking soda, and fine sea salt and stir with a rubber spatula until just combined. Fold in the chocolate.

3. Using a spring-loaded cookie scoop, a tablespoon, or two spoons, portion into 2-tablespoon balls of dough and arrange them on the baking sheets, spaced out by at least 3 inches because they'll spread as they bake. Top each one with a few more pieces of chocolate, if desired, and use your fingers or a spatula to flatten it slightly. Sprinkle each cookie with a small pinch of flaky salt.

4. Transfer a pan, one at a time, to the oven and bake until the cookies start to turn golden at the edges, 13 to 15 minutes.

5. Remove the pan from the oven and let the cookies cool for 10 minutes on the pan (meanwhile, bake off the second pan of cookies). Carefully transfer them to a wire rack to cool completely before eating. Packed in an airtight container, they'll keep for up to 3 days at room temperature or for 1 month in the freezer.

BOUGATSA CUPS
Custard Pie Bites

If you've ever eaten at a Greek restaurant, you might have been treated to a complimentary slice of bougatsa after your meal. It's one of our classic desserts, with its flaky, cinnamon-dusted phyllo concealing a just-set, creamy milk custard. It looks rich and heavy, but it's actually lighter than you might expect, since it's usually made with milk rather than cream. These bougatsa bites are easy to make at home, and I streamline the process by using frozen puff pastry instead of layering in buttered sheets of phyllo. And because they're assembled in muffin tins, they're easy to eat out of hand, too. The creamy filling is just sweet enough, making it a perfect after-dinner dessert or a treat to enjoy with your morning coffee.

Makes 12 bites
Ready in 45 minutes

3 large eggs
¾ cup granulated sugar
2 teaspoons vanilla extract
⅛ teaspoon fine sea salt
½ cup all-purpose flour, plus more for dusting
2 cups whole milk or half-and-half, at room temperature
1 cinnamon stick
1 thick strip lemon zest
Olive oil cooking spray, for greasing the muffin tins
1 sheet frozen puff pastry, thawed overnight in the refrigerator
Confectioners' sugar, for dusting
Ground cinnamon, for dusting

1. In a bowl, whisk together the eggs and granulated sugar until thoroughly combined and a bit lighter in color. Whisk in the vanilla and salt, followed by the flour. Gradually add the milk, whisking constantly to ensure a smooth consistency.

2. Scrape the mixture into a saucepan, add the cinnamon stick and lemon zest, and set over medium heat, whisking constantly. Watch carefully and as soon as steam starts to appear, turn down the heat if necessary to prevent boiling and continue cooking until the custard thickens to a puddinglike consistency, 6 to 10 minutes. Remove the pan from the heat. Pick out the cinnamon and lemon strip and let the custard cool while you prepare the crust.

3. Preheat the oven to 425°F. Lightly spray 12 cups of a standard muffin tin with the cooking spray.

4. On a lightly floured work surface, roll out the puff pastry thinly, to a thickness of between ¹⁄₁₆ and ⅛ inch. Use a 3½-inch round cutter or glass to create twelve thin rounds of pastry. (It can be helpful to roll them out once more after you cut them into rounds to make them slightly larger.) Press each one into a prepared muffin cup to form a crust that covers the bottom and up the side, pressing the pastry as far as you can above the edge to create as much room as possible for the filling.

5. Divide the custard among the cups, filling them almost all the way to the top. Transfer the tin to the oven and bake the cups until just set in the centers and lightly browned, 17 to 20 minutes.

6. Remove the tin from the oven and serve the bougatsa warm or at room temperature, dusted with confectioners' sugar and a few pinches of ground cinnamon. Packed in an airtight container, they'll keep for up to 3 days in the refrigerator.

MOM'S VASILOPITA
New Year's Day Yogurt Cake

Vasilopita is a classic cake for New Year's Day in Greece, and traditionally it's baked with a coin (called a flouri) hidden in the batter. The person who gets the coin in their slice can count on good luck for the year ahead! It's one of my all-time favorite desserts, and this is my mom's recipe, reflecting how she has always made it. A healthy amount of Greek yogurt keeps it tender and fluffy, with a rich, buttery flavor and bright citrus notes. Additionally, pomegranates have long been hugely symbolic throughout Greece, representing strength, fertility, and good fortune, and another New Year's Day custom is to smash a pomegranate at the front door of the house and make a wish. So in honor of that tradition, I always love to decorate this cake with them, too.

Serves 8
Ready in 45 minutes

Softened butter, for greasing the pan
3 large eggs, separated
1 (7-ounce) container whole milk Greek yogurt (1 scant cup)
8 tablespoons (1 stick) unsalted butter, melted and cooled
1 teaspoon vanilla extract
Grated zest of ½ orange
Grated zest of ½ lemon
1 cup confectioners' sugar, plus more for dusting
1 tablespoon baking powder
1 cup all-purpose flour
About ½ cup pomegranate airls, for decorating

1. Preheat the oven to 350°F. Lightly grease a 9-inch round cake pan or springform pan with the butter.

2. In a bowl, using a handheld electric mixer, beat the egg whites until they become frothy, about 30 seconds.

3. In a separate bowl, beat the yolks until they lighten in color, about 30 seconds. Scrape the yolks into the egg whites and add the yogurt, melted butter, vanilla, and citrus zests and beat until the mixture is creamy. Add the confectioners' sugar and mix until just incorporated. Quickly beat in the baking powder, then fold in the flour until no streaks remain. Scrape the batter into the prepared pan and smooth the surface using a rubber spatula.

4. Transfer the pan to the oven and bake until a toothpick tester comes out clean, 30 to 35 minutes.

5. Remove the pan from the oven and allow the cake to cool for 10 minutes in the pan, then unmold and cool it completely on a wire rack.

6. Just before serving, dust the cake with confectioners' sugar and decorate the surface with the pomegranate airls. Wrapped loosely, the cake will keep for up to 3 days at room temperature or for 1 month in the freezer, sealed in an airtight bag or container.

Change It Up
Make it gluten-free: Swap one-to-one gluten-free flour for the all-purpose flour.

PORTOKALOPITA
Orange Phyllo Cake

Another traditional Greek dessert, this phyllo cake originates from the island of Crete. It incorporates an orange syrup that's poured over the cooked cake, making it a bit sweeter than my typical desserts. But it's such a uniquely special, favorite dessert that I had to include it in this book. It may take a few steps, but it's a straightforward process and great for making ahead of time because the resting time helps it solidify and become easier to slice.

Makes 9 squares
Ready in 1 hour 10 minutes

Syrup
2 cups granulated sugar
1 cup water
¼ cup freshly squeezed orange juice
1 thick strip of orange zest
1 cinnamon stick

Cake
16 (14 by 18-inch, #4) frozen phyllo sheets (10 ounces), thawed overnight in the refrigerator
1 cup Greek olive oil, plus more for greasing the pan
1 cup granulated sugar
2 large eggs
Grated zest and juice of 2 oranges
½ cup whole milk Greek yogurt
2 teaspoons baking powder
1 teaspoon vanilla extract
Pinch of fine sea salt

Ice cream, for serving

1. To make the syrup: In a medium saucepan, combine all the ingredients and bring just to a boil over high heat, stirring often until the sugar has dissolved. Allow to cool, then pick out the orange zest and cinnamon stick.

2. To make the cake: Preheat the oven to 200°F.

3. Roll up the phyllo sheets into one long log and slice it crosswise into strips about 1 inch wide. Transfer the log to an unlined baking sheet and use your fingers to fluff and separate the strips as best you can.

4. Transfer the pan to the oven and bake until the phyllo strips are dried out, about 30 minutes, flipping them halfway through.

5. Remove the pan from the oven and set aside to cool.

6. Increase the oven temperature to 325°F. Lightly brush an 8 by 8-inch metal baking pan with oil.

7. In a large bowl, whisk together the oil and sugar. Add the eggs and beat until the mixture is smooth. Whisk in the orange zest and juice, the yogurt, baking powder, vanilla, and salt. Working a handful at a time, crumble the dried phyllo over the batter and stir it into the batter, making sure to stir with each addition to keep the phyllo from clumping. Scrape the batter into the prepared pan, smooth the surface, and tap the pan on the counter once or twice to remove any air bubbles.

8. Transfer the pan to the oven and bake until golden on top and set in the center, 35 to 40 minutes.

9. Remove the pan from the oven and immediately pour the syrup onto the cake. Allow the cake to set in the pan and cool completely.

10. Transfer the pan to the refrigerator until you're ready to serve (you can make the cake up to a day in advance). Wrapped loosely, the cake will keep for up to 3 days at room temperature or for 1 month in the freezer, sealed in an airtight bag or container.

11. When ready to serve, slice the cake into nine squares. Serve with ice cream on top or on the side.

FLEXIBLE PEANUT BUTTER–BANANA CHOCOLATE CHIP BARS

Here is one of my all-time most popular recipes on TikTok, and it's easy to know why: These dessert bars are packed with healthy ingredients; very low in sugar; made in a one-bowl, no-mixer operation; and can be ready to go into the oven in about 5 minutes. On top of that, you can make them with pretty much whatever you've got on hand! I've listed out many of my favorite variations below. Just note that it is extremely important to cool the bars completely before slicing; otherwise, they will be too moist. I typically make them a day in advance, so they have ample time to firm up overnight.

Makes 9 bars
Ready in 30 minutes

2 ripe bananas
1 cup natural peanut butter, at room temperature
¼ cup superfine almond flour
⅓ cup maple syrup or honey
1 large egg
1 teaspoon ground cinnamon
1 teaspoon baking soda
Pinch of fine sea salt
½ cup semisweet chocolate chips, plus more for topping

1. Preheat the oven to 325°F. Line an 8 by 8-inch metal baking pan with parchment paper.

2. In a large bowl, mash the bananas. Add the peanut butter, flour, maple syrup, egg, cinnamon, baking soda, and salt, and mix until evenly combined. Stir in the chocolate chips.

3. Scrape the batter into the prepared pan and smooth the surface. Sprinkle a few more chocolate chips on top and gently press them into the batter.

4. Transfer the pan to the oven and bake until a toothpick tester comes out clean, about 25 minutes.

5. Cool the bars completely in the pan, at least 2 hours and ideally overnight, before slicing. Once sliced, the bars will keep for up to 4 days in an airtight container in the refrigerator or for up to 1 month in the freezer.

Change It Up

Peanut Butter–Pumpkin Chocolate Chip Bars: Substitute ¾ cup pumpkin puree for the bananas.

Peanut Butter–Banana Brownies: Add 3 tablespoons cocoa powder to the batter and omit the cinnamon.

S'mores Bars: Reduce the almond flour to ⅓ cup and add 2 tablespoons coconut sugar to the batter. Fold in ½ cup mini marshmallows along with the chocolate chips, sprinkling a few more on top before baking.

Make it peanut-free: Substitute almond butter or any nut or seed butter for the peanut butter.

Easy swaps: Substitute oat flour or all-purpose flour for the almond flour.

Make it vegan: Substitute a flax egg (1 tablespoon flax meal whisked with 3 tablespoons water) for the egg.

INVISIBLE APPLE LOAF CAKE

This cake (called Gâteau Invisible in France, where it originated) gets its name because the apples are almost impossible to detect just from looking at it. They're very thinly sliced and stacked into the pan, then covered with a light, crepelike batter, so that in the oven, the two parts merge into one. You'll certainly taste them, though; that is why I've always loved this cake. The apples are so prominent in flavor that very little extra sugar is needed for it to taste properly sweet. Just be sure to choose sweet varieties of apples and avoid tart ones such as Granny Smiths.

Serves 8
Ready in 1 hour 10 minutes

- 3 large eggs
- ⅔ cup whole milk, slightly warmed
- 3 tablespoons unsalted butter, melted
- 1 teaspoon vanilla extract
- ½ cup all-purpose flour
- ½ cup confectioners' sugar, plus more for dusting
- ½ teaspoon ground cinnamon
- 1 teaspoon baking powder
- ¼ teaspoon fine sea salt
- 4 sweet apples (1½ to 2 pounds total), preferably Fuji, Honeycrisp, or Pink Lady

1. Preheat the oven to 350°F. Line a 9 by 5-inch loaf pan with parchment paper (see my parchment-lining tip on page 40).

2. In a large bowl, whisk together the eggs, milk, butter, and vanilla. Add the flour, confectioners' sugar, cinnamon, baking powder, and salt and mix until smooth. The batter will be on the thin side.

3. Peel and core the apples and then slice them *very* thinly on a mandoline—ideally about ¹⁄₁₆ inch thick. Add them to the batter and stir gently so that the apples are evenly coated.

4. Using your hands or a slotted spoon, lift the apples from the batter and layer them in the prepared pan in batches, gently flattening out each addition into a smooth layer. Pour the remaining batter over the apples.

5. Transfer the pan to the oven and bake the cake until the top is set in the center and a toothpick tester comes out mostly clean, 50 to 60 minutes. If you'd like a more golden-brown crust, place the pan under the broiler for 1 to 2 minutes, watching carefully. The cake will puff slightly in the oven but deflate as it cools.

6. Remove the pan from the oven and allow the cake to cool in the pan for 10 minutes, then, using the parchment, gently unmold it from the pan and cool for at least another 15 minutes on a wire rack before slicing. Sprinkle with a little confectioners' sugar if desired. Wrapped tightly, the cake will keep for up to 3 days in the refrigerator or for up to 1 month in the freezer.

Change It Up

Invisible Pear Cake: Substitute pears for the apples. Make sure they're ripe and sweet (and sliced very thinly!).

Make it gluten-free: Substitute one-to-one gluten-free flour for the all-purpose flour.

NO-BAKE BROWNIE CUPS

My yiayia and my papou used to sneak my brother and me a dollar when we were kids so we could run to the corner store to buy ourselves a candy bar treat. Those little adventures are some of my favorite memories growing up, and now it always makes me smile when my mom returns the favor, sneaking my kids little treats when she thinks I'm not looking. I always chose a simple chocolate bar on those excursions, and these brownie cups channel its simplicity—but with much less sugar and overall better ingredients. Keep these on hand as a perfect treat to satisfy a sweet craving.

Makes 10 brownie cups
Ready in 2 hours

2 cups superfine almond flour
½ cup maple syrup or honey
¼ cup natural cocoa powder
2 tablespoons creamy peanut butter, at room temperature

Chocolate Glaze
¼ cup creamy natural peanut butter, at room temperature
3 tablespoons semisweet chocolate chips (dairy-free, if necessary)
Cacao nibs or flaky sea salt, for garnish

1. Line 10 cups of a standard muffin tin with paper liners.

2. In a medium bowl, stir together the flour, maple syrup, cocoa powder, and peanut butter until smooth. Divide the mixture equally among the prepared muffin cups, pressing down on each one to form an even thickness.

3. To make the glaze: In a small saucepan over low heat, combine the peanut butter and chocolate chips and stir until the mixture is smooth. While it's warm, spoon the mixture over the brownie tops. Sprinkle each one with a pinch of cacao nibs.

4. Transfer the pan to the refrigerator for 2 hours, until firm. Packed in an airtight container, the cups will keep for up to 5 days in the refrigerator or for 1 month in the freezer.

Change It Up

To make it nut-free: Use sunflower seed butter instead of peanut butter. Substitute pumpkin seed or sunflower seed flour for the almond flour; you can make this by blending raw seeds in a high-powered blender until ground.

EASY COCONUT CAKE

For the same reason that I love my loaf pans, I find my 6-inch cake pans to be so handy for baking off an attractive but slightly smaller cake. This way, there's not a huge cake sitting around for several days. This coconut cake has a rich, satisfying texture and, like all my favorite desserts, uses nutrient-dense, minimally-processed ingredients and a relatively small amount of sugar. If you prefer a more pronounced coconut flavor, be sure to use "virgin" or unrefined coconut oil. And if you don't feel like including the frosting, the cake is also great with a simple dusting of confectioners' sugar.

Serves 6 to 8
Ready in 1 hour

Cake
Olive oil cooking spray, for greasing the pan
2 large eggs
⅓ cup maple syrup or honey
¼ cup whole milk Greek yogurt
1 teaspoon vanilla or almond extract
¼ cup coconut oil, melted and cooled
1¾ cups superfine almond flour
¼ cup coconut flour
½ teaspoon baking soda
½ teaspoon baking powder
¼ teaspoon fine sea salt

Cream Cheese Frosting
4 ounces cream cheese, at room temperature
½ cup confectioners' sugar
½ teaspoon vanilla or almond extract

2 tablespoons toasted, unsweetened shredded coconut, for sprinkling

1. To make the cake: Preheat the oven to 350°F. Lightly spray a 6-inch round cake pan or springform pan with the cooking spray and line the bottom with parchment paper.

2. In a bowl, whisk together the eggs, maple syrup, yogurt, and vanilla until smooth. Whisk in the oil. Add the two flours, the baking soda, baking powder, and salt, mixing until a thick batter forms. Scrape it into the prepared pan and press it into an even layer.

3. Transfer the pan to the oven and bake the cake until a toothpick tester comes out clean, 25 to 30 minutes.

4. Remove the pan from the oven and let the cake cool in the pan for 5 minutes, then unmold it onto a wire rack to cool completely before frosting.

5. To make the frosting: In a bowl, using a handheld electric mixer, beat together the cream cheese, confectioners' sugar, and vanilla until smooth and light.

6. Spread the frosting evenly over the top of the cooled cake and sprinkle with the coconut. Wrapped loosely, the cake will keep for 3 days at room temperature or for up to 1 month in the freezer in an airtight bag or container.

Change It Up

Make it dairy-free: Use nondairy yogurt (such as coconut yogurt) in the cake and vegan cream cheese in the frosting.

FIVE-MINUTE SANGRIA SLUSHIE

I don't drink cocktails very often, but for an adults-only BBQ, I love to mix up this quick, light, and quenching blender drink. Use seasonal fruits you've frozen yourself or store-bought bagged frozen fruits. Since it's always picked in season and flash-frozen, the store-bought fruit is a great option and often more flavorful than its fresh counterpart. You can blend this up and enjoy it right away, serving it out of wine or margarita glasses, or put the blended mixture in the freezer. Because of the alcohol, it won't freeze solid and will instead become a granita-like dessert to eat with a spoon.

Serves 4
Ready in 5 minutes

2 cups frozen mango chunks
2 cups frozen strawberries
2 cups rosé, pinot grigio, Sauvignon Blanc, or Chardonnay
¼ cup maple syrup or honey
1 tablespoon fresh lime or lemon juice
Mint leaves, for garnish
Lime wedges, for garnish

In a high-powered blender, combine the frozen fruits, wine, maple syrup, and lime juice and pulse until the mixture is smooth. You can enjoy this right away as a slushie, garnished with the mint and lime. (Alternatively, freeze the mixture in a loaf pan until it's set, about 6 hours, and serve in ice cream bowls as more of a granita.)

Change It Up

Make it a mocktail: Substitute 1 cup cranberry juice and 1 cup orange juice for the wine. Without the alcohol, the mixture will freeze solid, so allow it to defrost partially and then reblend to create a slushie texture before serving.

Easy swaps: Frozen peaches, watermelon, blueberries, nectarines, cherries, or raspberries can all be swapped in for the mango and strawberries.

NUTRITIONAL INFORMATION

Nutritional information listed is per serving or portion and does not factor in suggested toppings, condiments, or accompaniments. If the recipe yield is listed as a range, the information below reflects the average of the range. These data have been calculated using information from the U.S. Department of Agriculture (USDA) database but should only be considered an estimate or approximation of the nutritional content of a recipe, due to numerous factors (such as type of brand, method of measurement, or fluctuations of whole ingredients) that can determine the nutritional makeup of any ingredient or recipe.

	Calories	Protein (g)	Fat (g)	Carbs (g)
A				
Air-Fryer Artichoke Bites with Aioli	136	5	4	22
Arakas (Braised Sweet Peas with Artichokes & Chickpeas)	584	19	37	50
Avgolemono (Lemony Chicken Soup)	580	56	23	30
B				
Baba's Grain-Free Pancakes	496	21	35	27
Baked Egg Tortilla with Ham & Beans	349	22	19	23
Baked Halloumi & Gouda in Puff Pastry	402	15	29	18
Balsamic Roasted Strawberries with Whipped Honey-Ricotta	225	8	12	24
Banana-Oat Bread with Blueberries	162	7	7	34
Bougatsa Cups (Custard Pie Bites)	278	5	13	35
Boyfriend Steak Skillet with Peppers & Feta	626	44	43	16
Breakfast Biscuit Loaf	316	7	15	16
Broccoli-Feta Bake with Pasta	618	21	33	60
Broccoli-Feta Soup	341	17	9	54
Broccoli Kaltsounia (Broccoli Hand Pies)	385	13	21	37
Brussels Sprouts Salad with Halloumi, Dates & Crispy Shallots	401	11	28	34
C				
Cauliflower Steaks Parmesan	286	11	20	20
Cauliflower Wedge Salad with Bacon & Blue Cheese Dressing	471	16	40	18
Chicken Fasolakia (Green Bean Stew)	668	61	39	26
Chicken Saganaki	684	57	40	21
Chili-Lime Shrimp "Tacos" with Pineapple Salsa	359	31	19	18
Chocolate Chip & Banana Breakfast Cookies	114	2	8	9
Cocoa Dutch Baby with Fresh Strawberries	332	12	19	29

	Calories	Protein (g)	Fat (g)	Carbs (g)
Creamy Lemon Shrimp & Zucchini	441	44	22	12
Creamy Sheet Pan Gnocchi	259	8	16	24
Creamy Zucchini & White Bean Soup	330	19	8	48
Crispy Feta-Stuffed Olives	151	5	10	11
Crispy Parmesan Carrot Sticks	216	8	14	16
Crispy Shallots	79	1	5	7
Crunchy Baked Beef Souvlaki Tacos	244	46	38	24
Crunchy Potato Schiacciata	139	4	5	19
D-E				
Deconstructed Gemista (Deconstructed Rice & Vegetable-Stuffed Peppers)	526	37	23	41
Diner Cheeseburger Bites	233	14	19	1
Easier Skillet Moussaka	585	27	34	46
Easy Coconut Cake	403	9	31	26
Easy Lemon-Garlic-Parmesan Chicken	435	44	26	5
Easy Lemony Hummus	165	6	10	16
Elina's Pumpkin–Chocolate Chip Muffins	272	7	15	28
Epic Meat Lasagna	838	63	29	80
F-G				
Fáva (Greek Split Pea Soup)	609	26	27	70
Five-Minute Sangria Slushie	237	1	0	39
Flexible Peanut Butter–Banana Chocolate Chip Bars	309	10	21	25
Fresh Zucchini Noodle Salad	213	3	20	8
Garidopetoules (Shrimp Fritters)	138	12	9	3
Garlic Aioli	258	1	28	1
Greek Lamb Fricassee	519	71	22	14
Greek Layered Potato Bake	402	9	26	35
H-I-K				
Halibut Kleftiko (Pesto Halibut Baked in Parchment)	404	40	24	7
Herby Ricotta Dumplings in Vegetable Soup	663	32	43	41
Homemade Yogurt Flatbreads	221	12	13	24
Honey-Balsamic Roasted Beets	152	2	7	22
Honey-Butter Orange Roasted Chicken with Root Vegetables	690	38	43	40
Honey-Roasted Salmon-Farro Bowls with Radishes & Broccolini	482	38	25	28

	Calories	Protein (g)	Fat (g)	Carbs (g)
Horiatiki (Classic Greek Salad over White Bean–Feta Dip)	321	11	27	13
Invisible Apple Loaf Cake	176	4	7	26
L				
Ladenia (Greek Village Pizza)	291	6	10	45
Lahanopita Strifti (Spiral Pie with Cabbage & Feta)	302	8	21	23
Lazy Spanakopita	175	7	11	11
Lazy Tzatziki	28	1	2	1
Leek & Zucchini Scarpaccia	277	7	9	42
Lemony Orzotto with Spinach & Peas	495	21	19	61
Lighter Baklava Cheesecake Bars	245	7	14	24
Loaf Pan Chicken Gyros	438	56	21	2
Low-Carb Chicken Nuggets with Crispy Baked French Fries	546	54	32	10
M				
Mama's Juicy Fruit Salad	154	2	1	37
Mediterranean Baked Cod	275	35	13	3
Mediterranean Meatloaf	534	43	29	24
Mediterranean Tortellini Salad	700	27	44	50
Mediterranean Turkey-Crust Pizza	330	42	14	9
Mediterranean Veggie Stir-Fry	183	7	13	12
Melitzanosalata Garlic Bread	361	11	20	29
Micro Chop Salad with Goddess Dressing	910	13	76	54
Mom's Vasilopita (New Year's Day Yogurt Cake)	247	5	14	26
N-O-P				
No-Bake Brownie Cups	239	7	17	20
No-Bake Strawberry Tiramisu	319	5	15	43
Portokalopita (Orange Phyllo Cake)	542	4	29	37
One-Pan Chicken with Orzo, Sun-Dried Tomatoes & Mozzarella	742	74	30	43
R				
Roasted Butternut Squash with Tahini-Lime Sauce	407	10	28	52
Roasted Garlic Girl Soup	476	13	25	53
Roasted Pesto Cabbage Wedges	196	4	16	11
Roasted Veggie "Pizza"	242	14	14	17

	Calories	Protein (g)	Fat (g)	Carbs (g)
S				
Seared Scallops over Creamy Zucchini Couscous	748	42	31	75
Sesame-Crusted Baked Feta with Hot Honey	184	9	12	
Sheet Pan Chicken Caponata	831	65	50	31
Smashed Broccoli Chips	336	23	20	17
Smoky Spanish Lentil Soup with Chorizo	348	20	19	25
Soutzoukakia (Baked Greek Meatballs & Potatoes)	879	49	51	54
Special Sauce	163	0	16	6
Spiced Roasted Asparagus over Burrata	396	17	33	13
Spicy Mayo	33	0	3	0
Spicy Mayo Sauce	192	0	20	2
Spicy Poached Salmon	435	39	25	13
Spicy Ranch Dip	195	1	21	1
Spicy Salmon-Rice Muffins	85	8	5	2
Spinach & Feta Cookies	102	4	6	8
Spinach & Feta Stuffed Salmon	349	39	19	4
Summery Pita Salad with Figs, Peaches, Tomatoes & Corn	334	7	22	31
T-V				
Tahini-Crusted Chickpeas	250	11	12	28
The Ultimate Cobb Salad	957	49	71	37
Tuna Tostadas	221	17	9	19
Vegan Tahini–Chocolate Chunk Cookies	212	3	14	20
Vegetable-Stuffed Chicken Breasts	526	66	25	7
Vegetable-Stuffed Portobellos	312	18	22	13
Veggie Egg Bites with Feta & Olives	117	8	8	3
Veggie Quiche in a Smashed Potato Crust	229	12	12	18
W-Y-Z				
Warm Winter Vegetable Salad with Quinoa	448	8	25	50
Yiannis's Favorite Pork Souvlaki Wraps	563	66	16	37
Yiayia's Maroulosalata (Romaine Salad with Scallions & Dill)	377	8	34	14
Yogurt Flatbreads	228	9	4	38
Zucchini & Prosciutto "Lasagna" Loaf	323	27	19	14

NUTRITIONAL INFORMATION

ACKNOWLEDGMENTS

Were it not for my Hungry Happens community, this book would have never happened. Your feedback, encouragement, and mutual love for cooking healthy dishes have been a constant source of motivation. Thank you for trying my recipes and for sharing your experiences with me. This cookbook is a celebration of our shared passion, and I hope these recipes bring you and your loved ones joy and happy bellies, like they did ours!

Thank you to my parents, Katerina and Panagiotis, whose unwavering support and love have led me here. Thank you for always showing up for me when it really mattered. Thank you for being extraordinary role models and demonstrating to me that you can succeed against all odds. Thank you for always being my biggest cheerleaders (honest recipe criticism—delivered kindly) and for sharing your wisdom and recipes with me.

Lukas Volger, I'm so lucky and grateful to have had you by my side throughout this process. Your talent and dedication have transformed my ideas into a beautifully crafted cookbook that I am so proud of. It would not be what it is without your expertise.

Susan Roxborough, your keen guidance, thoughtful feedback, and unwavering support have been instrumental in shaping this cookbook. Thank you for believing in me and my vision from the get-go.

Antonis Achilleos, your talent, skill, and intuition have truly elevated this cookbook. We aligned instantly on the vision and by day two of the photo shoot, we were finishing each other's sentences. Thank you for working diligently to make this project one of a kind—you knocked it out of the park!

Monica Pierini, thank you for indulging my raccoon-garnish tendencies. But seriously, your artistry and attention to detail have transformed each recipe into a visual masterpiece. Thank you for your unwavering hard work, which turned every photo into a feast for the eyes.

Paige Hicks, thank you for bringing laughter and great energy to the photo shoot every day. From selecting the perfect plates to arranging the ideal backdrop, your prop styling talent brought my recipes to life in ways I never imagined.

Alyssa Kondrack, your enthusiasm, technique, and hard work were invaluable on those long shoot days. Thank you for your dedication, artistry, and ability to make every dish shine.

Julie Bishop, you transcended my expectations by testing these recipes so quickly and efficiently. It was such a pleasure to receive your feedback.

Thank you, Ian Dingman, for designing a visually gorgeous book that I can proudly share with my community, family, and friends.

Thank you to production editor Ashley Pierce, production manager Kelli Tokos, managing editor Alexandra Fox, editorial assistant Elaine Hennig, marketer Kristin Casemore, and publicist Chloe Aryeh for the time and care you put into producing my cookbook and bringing it to readers. I appreciate all your efforts.

To my loving children, thank you for being my biggest supporters and taste testers throughout this journey. Elina, you have been by my side every step of the way, helping me in the kitchen, testing the recipes, and cleaning up endless dishes. I am so lucky you love to cook as much as I do! Yiannis, you are always there to boost my confidence and help motivate me to keep going (even when I feel like giving up). This cookbook is dedicated to you both as it reflects the love we share for food and family. I hope it inspires you to continue your culinary adventures with your own families one day and keep cooking healthy at home! I love you, my babies!

INDEX

A
Aioli, 60
Air-Fryer Artichoke Bites with Aioli, 60
Apple Loaf cake, Invisible, 237
Arakas, 120
artichoke(s)
    Bites with Aioli, Air Fryer, 60
    Braised Sweet Peas with, & Chickpeas, 120
    Euro Tortellini Salad, 161
asparagus
    Spiced Roasted, over Burrata, 204
    Spicy Poached Salmon, 141
Avgolemono, 123
avocado
    Pineapple Salsa, 174
    Seaside Tuna Tostadas, 173
    Yogurt Flatbreads with Smoked Salmon, Avocado & Tzatziki, Homemade, 29

B
Baba's Grain-Free Pancakes with Easy Fruit Compote, 34
bacon
    Cauliflower Wedge Salad with, & Blue Cheese Dressing, 215
    Breakfast Biscuit Loaf, 46
    Diner Cheeseburger Bites with Special Sauce, 59
    Fall Brussels Sprouts Salad with Halloumi, Dates & Crispy Shallots, 212
Baklava Cheesecake Bars, Lighter, 225
Balsamic Roasted Strawberries with Whipped Honey-Ricotta, 55
banana
    Chocolate Chip & Banana Breakfast Cookies, 33
    Flexible Peanut Butter-Banana Chocolate Chip Bars, 234
bars. See cookies and bars
Basil Pesto, 199
    Creamy Sheet Pan Gnocchi with, 145
    Halibut Kleftiko with, 116
    Herby Ricotta Dumplings in Vegetable Soup with, 158
    Roasted Pesto Cabbage Wedges with, 199
beans
    Baked Egg Tortilla with Ham &, 38
    Creamy Zucchini & White Bean Soup, 181
    White Bean–Feta Whip, 208
    White Bean Soup, Creamy Zucchini &, 181
beans, green. See Green Bean Stew
Béchamel, 107
beef
    Boyfriend Steak Skillet with Peppers & Feta, 82
    Diner Cheeseburger Bites with Special Sauce, 59
    Lasagna, Epic Meat, 149

Meatballs & Potatoes, Baked, 111
Mediterranean Meatloaf, 94
Moussaka, Easier Skillet, 107
Souvlaki Tacos, Crunchy Baked, 89
Beets, Honey-Balsamic Roasted, 207
berries, in Easy Fruit Compote, 34. *See also specific berries*
blackberries, in Mama's Juicy Fruit Salad, 222
blueberries
    Banana-Oat Bread with, 41
    Mama's Juicy Fruit Salad, 222
blue cheese
    dressing, 215
    The Ultimate Cobb Salad, 186
Bougatsa Cups, 229
Bowls, Honey-Roasted Salmon-Farro with Radishes & Broccolini, 86
Boyfriend Steak Skillet with Peppers & Feta, 82
bread
    Garlic Bread, Cheesy, Topped with Greek Eggplant Dip, 56. *See also* flatbreads; quick bread
Bread Crumbs, Seasoned, 195
broccoli
    Chips, Smashed, with Spicy Ranch Dip, 63
    -Feta Pasta Bake, 150
    -Feta Soup, 98
    Hand Pies, 127
    Mediterranean Veggie Stir-Fry, 203
    Vegetable-Stuffed Chicken Breasts, 166
    Warm Winter Vegetable Salad with Quinoa, 97
Broccolini, Honey-Roasted Salmon-Farro Bowls with Radishes &, 86
Brownie Cups, No-Bake, 238
Burrata, Spiced Roasted Asparagus over, 204

C

cabbage
    & Feta, Spiral Pie with, 129
    Micro Chop Salad with Goddess Dressing, 185
    Roasted Pesto Cabbage Wedges, 199
cake
    Easy Coconut, 241
    Invisible Apple Loaf Cake, 237
    New Year's Day Yogurt Cake, 230
    Orange Phyllo, 233
capers, in Sheet Pan Chicken Caponata, 137
Caponata, Sheet Pan Chicken, 137
carrots
    Crispy Parmesan Carrot Sticks with Lazy Tzatziki, 200
    Honey-Butter Orange Roasted Chicken with Root Vegetables, 138
cauliflower
    Steaks Parmesan, 196
    Warm Winter Vegetable Salad with Quinoa, 97
    Wedge Salad with Bacon & Blue Cheese Dressing, 215
cheddar cheese
    Breakfast Biscuit Loaf, 46
    Crunchy Baked Beef Souvlaki Tacos, 89
cheese, 19. *See also specific cheeses*
    Cheesy Garlic Bread Topped with Greek Eggplant Dip, 56
    Cheeseburger Bites with Special Sauce, Diner, 59
    Cheesecake Bars, Lighter Baklava, 225
Cheesy Garlic Bread Topped with Greek Eggplant Dip, 56
chicken
    Caponata, Sheet-Pan, 137
    Fasolakia, 104
    Honey-Butter Orange Roasted, with Vegetables, 138

Lemon-Garlic-Parmesan, Easy, 78
Lemony Chicken Soup, 123
Loaf Pan Chicken Gyros, 103
Nuggets, Low-carb, with Crispy Baked French Fries, 165
Orzo with Sun-Dried Tomatoes & Mozzarella, One-Pan, 142
Saganaki, 77
The Ultimate Cobb Salad, 186
Vegetable-Stuffed Chicken Breasts, 166
chickpeas
    Braised Sweet Peas with Artichokes &, 120
    Easy Lemon Hummus, 108
    Tahini-Crusted, 68
Chili-Lime Shrimp "Tacos" with Pineapple Salsa, 120
chocolate
    Chocolate Chip & Banana Breakfast Cookies, 33
    Chocolate Chip Bars, Flexible Peanut Butter-Banana, 234
    Chocolate Chunk Cookies, Vegan Tahini-, 226
    Elina's Pumpkin-Chocolate Chip Muffins, 45
    Glaze, 238
    No-Bake Brownie Cups, 238
Chop Salad, Micro, with Goddess Dressing, 185
Chorizo, Smoky Spanish Lentil Soup with, 153
Coastal Baked Cod, 90
Cobb Salad, The Ultimate, 186
Cocoa Dutch Baby with Fresh Strawberries, 37
Coconut Cake, Easy, 241
Cod, Coastal Baked, 90
cookies and bars
    Chocolate Chip & Banana Breakfast Cookies, 33
    Lighter Baklava Cheesecake Bars, 225
    Peanut Butter-Banana Chocolate Chip Bars, Flexible, 234
    Spinach & Feta Cookies, 71
    Vegan Tahini-Chocolate Chunk Cookies, 226

cooking rules, 23
Corn, Summery Pita Salad with Figs, Peaches, Tomatoes &, 211
cottage cheese
- Epic Meat Lasagna, 149
- Lighter Baklava Cheesecake Bars, 225
Couscous, Creamy Zucchini, Seared Scallops with, 93
cream cheese
- Frosting, 241
- Lighter Baklava Cheesecake Bars, 225
Crispy Shallots, 212
Custard Pie Bites, 229

D

daily health tips, 25
daily meals, author's, 20
dairy, whole milk, 19. See also cottage cheese; yogurt
dates, 19
- Fall Brussels Sprouts Salad with Halloumi, & Crispy Shallots, 212
Deconstructed Gemista, 115
Deconstructed Rice & Vegetable Stuffed Peppers, 115
Dill, Romaine Salad with Scallions &, 216
Diner Cheeseburger Bites with Special Sauce, 59
dip(s)
- Aioli, 60
- Greek Eggplant, 56
- Spicy Ranch, 63
dressing. See also sauce; vinaigrette
- Blue Cheese, 215
- Goddess, 185
- tahini, 97
Dumplings, Herby Ricotta, in Vegetable Soup, 158
Dutch Baby, Cocoa, with Fresh Strawberries, 37

E

eggplant
- Dip, 56
- Easier Skillet Moussaka, 107
- Sheet Pan Chicken Caponata, 137
egg(s), 18
- Custard Pie Bites, 229
- Tortilla with Ham & Beans, Baked, 38
- The Ultimate Cobb Salad, 186
- Veggie Egg Bites with Feta & Olives, 30
- Veggie Quiche in a Smashed Potato Crust, 42
Elina's Pumpkin-Chocolate Chip Muffins, 45
Epic Meat Lasagna, 149
Euro Tortellini Salad, 161

F

Fall Brussels Sprouts Salad with Hallouomi, Dates & Crispy Shallots, 212
farro
- Honey-Roasted Salmon-Farro Bowls with Radishes & Broccolini, 86
Fasolakia, chicken, 104
Fáva, 119
feta, 17
- Boyfriend Steak Skillet with Peppers &, 82
- Broccoli-Feta Pasta Bake, 150
- Broccoli-Feta Soup, 98
- Chicken Saganaki, 77
- Greek Layered Potato Bake, 195
- Lazy Spanakopita, 124
- Romaine Salad with Scallions & Dill, 216
- Sesame-Crusted Baked, with Hot Honey, 52
- Spiced Tahini Squash with Lime &, 192
- Spinach & Feta Cookies, 71
- Spinach & Feta Stuffed Salmon, 170
- Spiral Pie with Cabbage &, 129
- -Stuffed Olives, Crispy, 767
- Veggie Egg Bites with, & Olives, 30
- White Bean–Feta Whip, 208

Figs, Summery Pita Salad with, Peaches, Tomatoes, & Corn, 211
fish and seafood
- Cod, Coastal Baked
- Halibut Kleftiko, 116
- Salmon-Farro Bowls, Honey-Roasted, with Radishes & Broccolini, 86
- Salmon-Rice Muffins, Spicy, 72
- Salmon, Spicy Poached, 141
- Salmon, Spinach & Feta Stuffed, 170
- Scallops, Seared, over Creamy Zuccchini Couscous, 93
- Smoked Salmon, Avocado & Tzatziki, Homemade Yogurt Flatbreads with, 29
- Shrimp & Zucchini, Creamy Lemon
- Shrimp Fritters, 51
- Shrimp "Tacos" Chili Lime, with Pineapple Salsa
- Tuna Tostadas, Seaside, 173
Five-Minute Sangria Slushie, 242
flatbreads
- Crunchy Potato Schiacciata, 154
- Yiannis's Favorite Pork Souvlaki Wraps, 108
- Yogurt Flatbreads with Smoked Salmon, Avocado & Tzatziki, Homemade, 29
Flour, Homemade Self-Rising, 71
French Fries, Crispy Baked, 165
Fricassee, Greek Lamb, 112
Fritters, Shrimp, 51
Frosting, Cream Cheese, 241. See also Glaze, Chocolate
fruit. See also specific types
- Compote, Easy, 34
- Salad, Mama's Juicy, 222

G

Garidopetoules, 51
garlic, 17
- Bread, Melitzanosalata, 56
- Roasted Garlic Girl Soup, 182
Gemista, Deconstructed, 115
Glaze, Chocolate, 238
Gnocchi, Creamy Sheet Pan, 145

Goddess Dressing, 185
gouda
    Baked Halloumi &, in Puff Pastry, 64
    Cheesy Garlic Bread Topped with Greek Eggplant Dip, 56
    Vegetable-Stuffed Portobellos, 178
Grain-Free Pancakes with Easy Fruit Compote, Baba's, 34
grains. See couscous; farro; orzo
Greek Layered Potato Bake, 195
Greek pantry, 17–18
Greek Salad over White Bean–Feta Whip, Classic, 208
gruyère, in Vegetable-Stuffed Portobellos, 178
Gyros, Loaf Pan Chicken, 103

H

Halibut Kleftiko, 116
Halloumi
    Fall Brussels Sprouts Salad with, Dates & Crispy Shallots, 212
    & Gouda, Baked, in Puff Pastry, 64
Ham, Baked Egg Tortilla with, & Beans, 38. See also prosciutto
Hand Pies, Broccoli, 127
health-forward pantry, 18–19
health rules, 24
health tips, daily, 25
herbs, 17
    Herby Ricotta Dumplings in Vegetable Soup, 158
honey, 18
    -Balsamic Roasted Beets, 207
    -Butter Orange Roasted Chicken with Root Vegetables, 138
    -Roasted Salmon-Farro Bowls with Radishes & Broccolini, 86
    Sesame-Crusted Baked Feta with Hot Honey, 52
Horiatiki, 208
Hot Honey, Sesame-Crusted Baked Feta with, 52
Hummus, Easy Lemon, 108

I

ingredients. See Greek pantry; health-forward pantry
Invisible Apple Loaf Cake, 237

J

jalapeño peppers
    Pineapple Salsa, 174
    Spicy Poached Salmon, 141

K

Kaltsounia, Broccoli, 127
Ketchup, Spicy, 165
Kleftiko, Halibut, 116

L

Ladenia, 133
Lahanopita Strifti, 129
lamb
    Easier Skillet Moussaka, 107
    Fricassee, Greek, 112
    Mediterranean Meatloaf, 94
Lasagna, Epic Meat, 149
"Lasagna" Loaf, Zucchini & Prosciutto, 85
Lazy Spanakopita, 124
Lazy Tzatziki, 200
    Crispy Parmesan Carrot Sticks with, 200
    Homemade Yogurt Flatbreads with, 29
    Honey-Roasted Salmon-Farro Bowls with, 86
    Mediterranean Meatloaf with, 94
    Shrimp Fritters with, 51
    Yiannis's Favorite Pork Souvlaki Wraps with, 108
Leek & Zucchini Scarpaccia, 157
lemon(s), 17
    Lemony Chicken Soup, 123
    -Garlic-Parmesan Chicken, Easy, 78
    Hummus, Easy, 108
    Lemony Orzotto with Spinach & Peas, 146
    Shrimp & Zucchini, Creamy, 81
Lentil Soup with Chorizo, Smoky Spanish, 153
lime
    Crema, 174
    Spiced Tahini Squash with, & Feta, 192
Loaf Cake, Invisible Apple, 237
Loaf Pan Chicken Gyros, 103
Loaf, Zucchini & Prosciutto "Lasagna," 85

M

Mama's Juicy Fruit Salad, 222
mangoes
    Five-Minute Sangria Slushie, 242
    Mama's Juicy Fruit Salad, 222
Maroulosalata, Yiayia's, 216
mascarpone, in No-Bake Strawberry Tiramisu, 221
mayo
    Sauce, Spicy, 173
    Spicy, 72
Meatballs & Potatoes, Baked, 111
Meatloaf, Mediterranean, 94
Mediterranean Meatloaf, 94
Mediterranean Turkey-Crust Pizza, 169
Mediterranean Veggie Stir-Fry, 203
Melitzanosalata Garlic Bread, 56
melon, in Mama's Juicy Fruit Salad, 222
Mexican cheese blend
    Crunchy Baked Beef Souvlaki Tacos, 89
    Diner Cheeseburger Bites with Special Sauce, 59
    Vegetable-Stuffed Chicken Breasts, 166
Micro Chop Salad with Goddess Dressing, 185
Mom's Vasilopita, 230
Moussaka, Easier Skillet, 107
mozzarella
    Cheesy Garlic Bread Topped with Greek Eggplant Dip, 56
    Lazy Spanakopita, 124
    Mediterranean Turkey-Crust Pizza, 169
    One-Pan Chicken Orzo with Sun-Dried Tomatoes &, 142

mozzarella (cont.)
   Roasted Veggie "Pizza," 177
   Vegetable-Stuffed Chicken Breasts, 166
   Zucchini & Prosciutto "Lasagna" Loaf, 85
Muffins, Elina's Pumpkin-Chocolate Chip, 45
Muffins, Spicy Salmon-Rice, 72
mushrooms
   Creamy Sheet Pan Gnocchi, 145
   Roasted Veggie "Pizza," 177
   Vegetable-Stuffed Portobellos, 178

N

New Year's Day Yogurt Cake, 230
No-Bake Brownie Cups, 238
No-Bake Strawberry Tiramisu, 221
Noodle Salad, Fresh Zucchini, 191
nuts and seeds, 18
   Micro Chop Salad with Goddess Dressing, 185

O

olive oil, Greek, 17
olives, 18
   Coastal Baked Cod, 90
   Crispy Feta-Stuffed, 67
   Fresh Zucchini Noodle Salad, 191
   Halibut Kleftiko, 116
   Mediterranean Turkey-Crust Pizza, 169
   Veggie Egg Bites with Feta &, 30
One-Pan Chicken Orzo with Sun-Dried Tomatoes & Mozzarella, 142
onions. See Pickled Red Onions, Favorite
orange
   Phyllo Cake, 233
   Honey-Butter Orange Roasted Chicken with Root Vegetables, 138
orzo
   Lemony Chicken Soup, 123
   Lemony Orzotto with Spinach & Peas, 146
   One-Pan Chicken Orzo with Sun-Dried Tomatoes & Mozzarella, 142
   Orzotto with Spinach & Peas, Lemony, 146

P

Pancakes, Baba's Grain-Free, with Easy Fruit Compote, 34. See also Cocoa Dutch Baby with Fresh Strawberries
Panko Topping, Crunchy, 97
pantry ingredients. See Greek pantry; health-forward pantry
Parmesan
   Carrot Sticks, Crispy, with Lazy Tzatziki, 200
   Smashed Broccoli Chips with Spicy Ranch Dip, 63
pasta. See also orzo
   Broccoli-Feta Pasta Bake, 150
   Epic Meat Lasagna, 149
   Euro Tortellini Salad, 161
Peaches, Tomatoes & Corn, Summery Pita Salad with, 211
peanut butter
   -Banana Chocolate Chip Bars, Flexible, 234
   No-Bake Brownie Cups, 238
peas, split
   Greek Split Pea Soup, 119
peas, sweet
   Sweet Peas with Artichokes & Chickpeas, Braised, 120
   Lemony Orzotto with Spinach & Peas, 146
peppers. See also jalapeño peppers
   Boyfriend Steak Skillet with, & Feta, 82
   Mediterranean Veggie Stir-Fry, 203
   Roasted Veggie "Pizza," 177
   Vegetable Stuffed, Rice &, 115
pesto
   Cabbage Wedges, Roasted, 199
   Halibut Baked in Parchment, 116
Phyllo Cake, Orange, 233
Phyllo Crust, 225
Pickled Red Onions, Favorite, 119
   Chili-Lime Shrimp "Tacos" with, 174
   Fall Brussels Sprouts Salad with, 212
   Greek Split Pea Soup with, 119
   Homemade Yogurt Flatbreads with, 29
   Warm Winter Vegetable Salad with, 97
   Yiannis's Favorite Pork Souvlaki Wraps with, 108
Pie, Spiral, with Cabbage & Feta, 129
Pineapple Salsa, 174
Pita Salad, Summery, with Figs, Peaches, Tomatoes & Corn, 211
pizza
   Mediterranean Turkey-Crust, 169
   Greek Village, 133
"Pizza," Roasted Veggie, 177
pomegranate, in Micro Chop Salad with Goddess Dressing, 185
pork. See also bacon; Chorizo; Ham; prosciutto; salami
   Baked Meatballs & Potatoes, 111
   Epic Meat Lasagna, 149
   Pork Souvlaki Wraps, Yiannis's Favorite, 108
Portobellos, Vegetable-Stuffed, 178
Portokalopita, 233
potato(es)
   Bake, Greek Layered, 195
   Baked Meatballs &, 111
   Easier Skillet Moussaka, 107
   French Fries, Crispy Baked, 165
   Potato Schiacciata, Crunchy, 154
   Roasted Garlic Girl Soup, 182
   Veggie Quiche in a Smashed Potato Crust, 42
prosciutto
   Zucchini & Prosciutto "Lasagna" Loaf, 85
Prosecco, in No-Bake Strawberry Tiramisu, 221
puff pastry
   Baked Halloumi & Gouda in, 64
   Custard Pie Bites, 229
Pumpkin-Chocolate Chip Muffins, Elina's, 45

Q

Quiche, Veggie, in a Smashed Potato Crust, 42
quick bread
  Banana-Oat Bread with Blueberries, 41
  Breakfast Biscuit Loaf, 46
  Elina's Pumpkin-Chocolate Chip Muffins, 45
Quinoa, Warm Winter Vegetable Salad with, 97

R

raspberries, in Mama's Juicy Fruit Salad, 222
rice
  Spicy Salmon-Rice Muffins, 72
  & Vegetable Stuffed Peppers, Deconstructed, 115
ricotta
  Epic Meat Lasagna, 149
  Herby Ricotta Dumplings in Vegetable Soup, 158
  Whipped Honey Ricotta, 55
Roasted Garlic Girl Soup, 182
Roasted Pesto Cabbage Wedges, 199
Roasted Veggie "Pizza," 177
Romaine Salad with Scallions & Dill, 216

S

Saganaki, Chicken, 77
salad
  Cauliflower Wedge, with Bacon & Blue Cheese Dressing, 215
  Classic Greek over White Bean–Feta Whip, 208
  Euro Tortellini, 161
  Fall Brussels Sprouts, with Hallouomi, Dates & Crispy Shallots, 212
  Micro Chop, with Goddess Dressing, 185
  Romaine, with Scallions & Dill, 216
  Summer Pita, with Figs, Peaches, Tomatoes & Corn, 211
  The Ultimate Cobb, 186

salami, in Euro Tortellini Salad, 161
salmon
  Homemade Yogurt Flatbreads with Smoked Salmon, Avocado & Tzatziki, 29
  Honey-Roasted Salmon-Farro Bowls with Radishes & Broccolini, 86
  Spicy Poached, 141
  Spicy Salmon-Rice Muffins, 72
  Spinach & Feta Stuffed, 170
  Salsa, Pineapple, 174
Sangria Slushie, Five-Minute, 242
sauce. See also dressing; Pineapple Salsa
  Béchamel, 107
  Special Sauce, 59
sausage. See chorizo; salami
Scallops, Seared, over Creamy Zucchini Couscous, 93
Scarpaccia, Leek & Zucchini, 157
Schiacciata, Crunchy Potato, 154
seafood. See fish and seafood; shrimp
Seaside Tuna Tostadas, 173
Self-Rising Flour, Homemade, 71
Sesame-Crusted Baked Feta with Hot Honey, 52
shallots. See Crispy Shallots
Sheet Pan Chicken Caponata, 137
Sheet Pan Gnocchi, Creamy, 145
shrimp
  Creamy Lemon, & Zucchini, 81
  Fritters, 51
  "Tacos" with Pineapple Salsa, Chili-Lime, 174
Skillet Moussaka, Easier, 107
Slushie, Five-Minute Sangria, 241
Smashed Broccoli Chips with Spicy Ranch Dip, 63
Smoky Spanish Lentil Soup with Chorizo, 153
soup
  Broccoli-Feta, 98
  Greek Split Pea, 119
  Lemony Chicken, 123
  Roasted Garlic Girl Soup, 182
  Smoky Spanish Lentil, with Chorizo, 153
  Vegetable, 158
Soutzoukakia, 111

Souvlaki Wraps, Yiannis's Favorite Pork, 108
Spanakopita, Lazy, 124
Special Sauce, 59
spinach
  & Feta Cookies, 71
  & Feta Stuffed Salmon, 170
  Lazy Spanakopita, 124
  Lemony Orzotto with Spinach & Peas, 146
Spiral Pie with Cabbage & Feta, 129
squash. See winter squash; yellow squash; zucchini
steak
  Boyfriend Steak Skillet with Peppers & Feta, 82
stew
  Green Bean, 104
stir-fry dishes
  Boyfriend Steak Skillet with Peppers & Feta, 82
  Mediterranean Veggie Stir-Fry, 203
strawberry(ies)
  Balsamic Roasted, with Whipped Honey Ricotta, 55
  Cocoa Dutch Baby with Fresh, 37
  Five-Minute Sangria Slushie, 242
  Mama's Juicy Fruit Salad, 222
  Tiramisu, No-Bake, 221
summer squash. See yellow squash; zucchini
Summery Pita Salad with Figs, Peaches, Tomatoes & Corn, 211
Sun-Dried Tomatoes & Mozzarella, One-Pan Chicken Orzo with, 142
Sweet Peas with Artichokes & Chickpeas, Braised, 120
sweet potato
  Honey-Butter Orange Roasted Chicken with Root Vegetables, 138
  Warm Winter Vegetable Salad with Quinoa, 97
Syrup, Orange, 233

INDEX 255

T

Tacos, Crunchy Baked Beef Souvlaki, 89
"Tacos" with Pineapple Salsa, Chili-Lime Shrimp, 174
tahini, 19
- -Chocolate Chunk Cookies, Vegan, 226
- -Crusted Chickpeas, 68
- dressing, 97
- Spiced Tahini Squash with Lime & Feta, 192

Tiramisu, No-Bake Strawberry, 221
tomato(es)
- Epic Meat Lasagna, 149
- Greek Village Pizza, 133
- Mediterranean Turkey-Crust Pizza, 169
- One-Pan Chicken Orzo with Sun-Dried, & Mozzarella, 142
- Relish, 89
- Roasted Veggie "Pizza," 177
- Summery Pita Salad with Figs, Peaches, Tomatoes & Corn, 211

topping
- Crunchy Panko, 97

Tortellini Salad, Euro, 161
tortilla(s)
- Baked Egg, with Ham & Beans, 38
- Crunchy Baked Beef Souvlaki Tacos, 89

Tostadas, Seaside Tuna, 173
Tuna Tostadas, Seaside, 173
Turkey-Crust Pizza, Mediterranean, 169
tzatziki. See Lazy Tzatziki

U

The Ultimate Cobb Salad, 186

V

Vasilopita, Mom's, 230
Vegan Tahini-Chocolate Chunk Cookies, 226
vegetable(s). *See also specific vegetables*
- Honey Butter Orange Roasted Chicken with Root, 138
- Roasted Veggie "Pizza," 177
- -Stuffed Chicken Breasts, 166
- -Stuffed Portobellos, 178
- Veggie Egg Bites with Feta & Olives, 30
- Veggie Quiche in a Smashed Potato Crust, 42
- Veggie Stir-Fry, Mediterranean, 203

vegetable tart. See Leek & Zucchini Scarpaccia
Vinaigrette, 204

W

Wedge Salad, Cauliflower, with Bacon & Blue Cheese Dressing, 215
Whip, White Bean-Feta, 208
Whipped Honey-Ricotta, 55
white bean(s)
- –Feta Whip, 208
- Soup, Creamy Zucchini &, 181

wine, in Five-Minute Sangria Slushie, 242

winter squash
- Spiced Tahini Squash with Lime & Feta, 192
- Warm Winter Vegetable Salad with Quinoa, 97
- Winter Vegetable Salad with Quinoa, Warm, 97

Y

yellow squash, in Vegetable-Stuffed Portobellos, 178
Yiannis's Favorite Pork Souvlaki Wraps, 108
Yiayia's Maroulosalata, 216
yogurt
- Flatbreads with Smoked Salmon, Avocado & Tzatziki, Homemade, 29
- Lazy Tzatziki, 200
- New Year's Day Yogurt Cake, 230

Z

zucchini
- Creamy Lemon Shrimp &, 81
- Halibut Kleftiko, 116
- Leek & Zucchini Scarpaccia, 157
- & Prosciutto "Lasagna" Loaf, 85
- Seared Scallops over Creamy Zucchini Couscous, 93
- & White Bean Soup, Creamy, 181
- Zucchini Noodle Salad, Fresh, 191